Develop Maths

	Frequently asked questions for adults	2
LESSON 1	Using subtraction	5
LESSON 2	Calculating fractions of a whole number	13
LESSON 3	Finding the whole number from a fraction	21
LESSON 4	Simplifying fractions	29
LESSON 5	Rounding numbers and decimals	37
LESSON 6	Turning fractions into decimals and percentages	45
LESSON 7	Calculating probability	53
LESSON 8	Calculating ratios	61
LESSON 9	Calculating proportion	69
LESSON 10	Calculating volume	76
LESSON 11	Calculating the area of right-angled triangles and irregular shapes	85
LESSON 12	Reading information from graphs	92
LESSON 13	Multiplying larger numbers	102
LESSON 14	Finding averages and ranges	111
LESSON 15	Finding a percentage of a number	119
	Vocabulary builder	123
	Score sheet	126
	And finally…	126
	Answers	127

Frequently Asked Questions For Adults

What is this book about?

Develop Maths is in level two of the *Practise & Pass 11+* series. It is a workbook for students who are going to take an 11+ test or school entrance exam that includes a maths section. In it I help students further their knowledge of 10 key types of question they've already practised in level one of the series, and introduce them to 5 new question types that they might face in the test. I also provide 300 further original questions for them to practise.

I provide coaching for students throughout the book. I talk them through the whole process, from answering questions to helping them understand their mistakes, so that they have a firm understanding of the basics.

(Note: if they haven't already done so I highly recommend that your student work through level one of the series – Discover Maths – before starting this book.)

How do I use this book?

This book is divided into bite-sized lessons for the students to work through. Each lesson covers a specific type of question and is set up in the same way:

1 I explain the question type, giving the student an understanding of what they need to know.

2 I provide one or two worked examples to show how the question type is best tackled.

(Note: I recommend that an adult reads through the explanation and example(s) with the student to ensure they have a firm understanding of what is required. It is possible that the method I suggest is different to the one the student may have used at school. In this case talk to the student to make sure they use the method they are happiest with.)

3 When ready, the student should work through the first set of practice questions on their own and mark their answers on the answer sheet provided.

Important: unlike in level one, an adult should mark this set of questions, and all the questions in this book. The answers can be found on pages 127 and 128. You might want to cut these out of the book so the temptation for the student to take a peek is removed!

4 I provide a summary of what the student's score means and give hints on how to improve it, if needs be, and how to speed up their work.

(Note: the student should discuss any errors and talk through the hints with an adult so that any problems are dealt with straight away.)

5 Next, there is a second set of practice questions. The student shouldn't work on these until they understand why they made mistakes first-time around.

6 Finally there is a score sheet on page 126 which should be completed after each lesson to keep a record of progress. This can be used to identify the question types the student needs to practise more

(Note: occasionally I will include a question that hasn't been explained in the lesson. This is by design: the student will very likely come up against a question they are not familiar with in the actual test so it's important that they get used to applying the knowledge they have to work out the right answer.)

Why does this book feature multiple choice answers?

Multiple choice answers are becoming the most common format for the 11+ and entrance exams. This means that 4 or 5 possible answers are given for each question and they are presented to the student in a grid format. To answer the question correctly the student has to put a horizontal line in the empty box next to the correct answer.

⇨ It's important that students learn to use these grids correctly from the outset so that they avoid making common errors, such as marking answers in the wrong place or accidentally missing out questions.

⇨ Do make sure you find out from the examination centre whether the multiple choice format is to be used in the final exam so you are confident that the student is doing the right preparation.

When should the student start to prepare for the exam and how often should they practise?

The sooner the student starts to prepare for the exam the better. Realistically, I suggest there should be a full year's run-up to the test so that the student has a chance to practise as many of the subject areas and question types that might appear in the exam as possible without having to study for hours and hours each week. This means working through all three levels of the *Practise & Pass 11+* series (this book is in level two of the series) at a steady and realistic pace.

For this book I recommend students work at the pace of 2 lessons a week which means 7 to 8 weeks in total. However, if a student is able, there is nothing to stop them moving through the book more quickly.

What's the best way for a student to study?

⇨ It's important that the student gets used to a test-type environment so make sure there's a clear space to work in, with no distractions. This means the TV and all music should be switched off, the student should be sat at a table and there should be a clock in clear view so that they can time themselves.

⇨ Students should use a pencil to answer the questions and have an eraser and some scrap paper to hand which they can use for any workings out.

(Note: I highly recommend that the student avoid practising on the same days that they have school homework and that they also have other extra-curricular activities – this means they have other outlets for their energies and don't become overworked, stressed or too bored with the practice.)

How quickly should a student answer the questions?

As this book is in level two of the series, students should be used to most of the question types so I do expect them to be up to speed. They should follow the timings I have provided so that they work at a 'real time' pace. I have provided 'tips for speeding up' throughout the book to help with this. Typically in the actual maths exam they will have 50 minutes to answer 50 questions (although, do check this with the examination centre as timings can vary).

What score should the student be aiming for?

Remember that 11+ tests and entrance examinations are tough to pass. I have written this book to reflect that fact, so it is unlikely that the student will sail through the book scoring 100% in each lesson.

After the first set of practice questions in every lesson, I have given a target score for that particular question type – this is based on my experience of teaching them year on year and should help you assess how the student is doing, and what, if any, areas need work. I also include helpful tips on how students can improve, and would recommend they use the 'vocabulary builder' on page 123.

I should add that the scores here in no way indicate whether the student will definitely pass or fail the exam; they are only here as a guide.

What is the 'vocabulary builder'?

The 'vocabulary builder' exercise is an extra task to help improve the student's vocabulary. In addition to this, one of the best ways for students to help prepare for the examination is to read regularly. The better their vocabulary, the better they are likely to cope with the questions in the actual exam (this is true even for maths!).

What should I do once this book is completed?

I recommend that the student move on to level three of the series: *Practice Tests*. This provides full practice test papers for your child to work through so that they know exactly what to expect on test day.

LESSON 1 Using Subtraction

In this exercise, you'll learn about some of the many types of question that require you to use subtraction. For these questions, it's important that you work out the problem on paper. Trying to calculate the answer quickly using mental arithmetic often leads to mistakes. Many questions are designed to be awkward, so take the extra few seconds to set the work out and get it right. Let's look at an example.

Example

Anil and Sue collect stickers. If Anil has 803 and Sue has 586,
how many more stickers than Sue has Anil?

A common mistake that students make in the question above is to add the two numbers together because it has the word 'more'. But if you read the question carefully, you'll see that this is a comparison question. So what you need to find is the 'difference', and this means subtracting the smaller number from the larger.

$$\begin{array}{r} 8\,0\,3 \\ -5\,8\,6 \end{array}$$

Another common mistake is in the subtraction itself. Remember that if you don't have enough value in the units column, you must exchange and regroup. So in the units column here, 3 is less than 6 so you need to exchange with the column next to it before starting the subtraction.

$$\begin{array}{r} {}^{7}\,{}^{9}\\ 8\!\!\!/\,0\!\!\!/\,3 \\ -5\,8\,6 \end{array}$$

Since there are no tens, take 1 from the hundreds column leaving 7 hundreds and make 10 tens. Next, take 1 from the tens leaving 9 tens and place it in the units column to give you 13. Now you can do the subtraction.

$$\begin{array}{r} {}^{7}\,{}^{9}\\ 8\!\!\!/\,0\!\!\!/\,3 \\ -5\,8\,6 \\ \hline 2\,1\,7 \end{array}$$

So the final answer is <u>217</u>. You can check this is correct by adding it to 586. They should make 803 when added.

HELPFUL HINT

Remember the key words you need to watch out for in questions that require you to subtract:

- many
- much more
- greater
- larger than
- how many
- much fewer
- less
- smaller

LESSON 1 PART 1

My Time **My Score**

Now look at the questions below. Work out your answers on some scrap paper and then mark them on the answer sheet. You have 10 minutes to complete this task. Write the time you took in the box above once you've finished. Remember to get an adult to mark your answers. Then write your score in the box at the top of this page.

1. A factory made 2,038 cars in January and 798 cars in February. How many more cars did it make in January?

2. Look at the table below. How many more passengers did the bus carry on Tuesday than Friday?

Day	Passengers
Monday	238
Tuesday	345
Wednesday	109
Thursday	407
Friday	265

3. If a holiday to Majorca costs £508 and a holiday to Menorca costs £946, how much money can you save by going to Majorca?

4. How much higher is a mountain that is 20,038ft than a mountain which is 18,903ft?

5. Paula drank 233ml from a 1 litre bottle of water. How much water is left in the bottle?

6. If a plane has flown 2,305 miles out of 6,500 miles, how far has it still to travel?

7. Carla is 1m 56cm tall. How much taller is Bill, who is 1m 79cm?

8. How many more employees has an office with 108 staff than an office with only 39 staff?

9. By how many pages is a book of 309 pages smaller than a book with 470 pages?

10. A car which has travelled 39,101 miles has travelled how many miles more than a car that has gone 28,046 miles?

LESSON 1 PART 1: ANSWER SHEET

Mark your answer by putting a horizontal line in 1 of the boxes, as in the example below.

Example:

383 ☐
217 ▬
723 ☐
223 ☐
287 ☐

1
2,836 ☐
5,958 ☐
6,058 ☐
1,240 ☐
2,760 ☐

2
1,364 ☐
610 ☐
80 ☐
120 ☐
142 ☐

3
£442 ☐
£848 ☐
£348 ☐
£448 ☐
£438 ☐

4
18,935ft ☐
1,135ft ☐
8,135ft ☐
2,135ft ☐
38,941f ☐

5
1,233ml ☐
233ml ☐
1,330ml ☐
767ml ☐
133ml ☐

6
8,805 miles ☐
4,205 miles ☐
5,205 miles ☐
4,105 miles ☐
4,195 miles ☐

7
135cm ☐
435cm ☐
23cm ☐
123cm ☐
223cm ☐

8
147 ☐
131 ☐
71 ☐
69 ☐
39 ☐

9
161 ☐
779 ☐
179 ☐
109 ☐
170 ☐

10
11,145 miles ☐
1,145 miles ☐
1,155 miles ☐
11,055 miles ☐
11,155 miles ☐

How Did You Do? Let's Find Out!

Remember, there is no self-marking in this book. Please get an adult to mark your answers.

If you scored 9 or more out of 10

These questions are really quite straightforward provided you are careful and don't rush. While 9 is a good score you should try to get 10 out of 10 on the next set of questions. Check where you went wrong and look at the further hints below before you move on.

If you scored fewer than 9 out of 10

Check the questions you got wrong and make sure you understand how to apply the method before you move on. Also check that you didn't make a mistake when putting your answers on the sheet. Read the further hints below and the tips for speeding up before moving on to the next set of questions.

Further hints

⇨ Did you notice that question 2 was set out in table form? This isn't unusual, and you need to be prepared for questions requiring you to read information correctly from a bar graph or table before you do the sum. (Lesson 12 will cover this in more detail.) Watch out for these and make sure you write down the correct numbers before you do your calculation!

⇨ Watch out for negative numbers. These often occur in questions about temperatures. If you're required to take away more than you have, simply reverse the numbers, do your subtraction and then put a negative (–) in front of your answer.

Example

If it is 9°C in Moscow and the temperature drops by 12°C, what is the new temperature?

This should be 9 – 12. Instead, reverse the numbers so it reads 12 – 9, which gives you 3. Now put a – sign in front of your answer so it reads –3°C, which is the answer you should mark on your answer grid. This way, it's easy to do these sums and it works every time!

TIPS FOR SPEEDING UP

- Did you subtract correctly? Did you remember the method of how to exchange the numbers in those questions where it was needed?

- Many students think that they can speed up by calculating problems mentally (in their head). I'd advise you not to do this – it'll make you more likely to make a mistake, especially when under pressure in an exam.

- Set your work out neatly in numbered order on your working paper – besides reducing the chance of making a mistake, it'll be easier for you to check your answers at the end.

LESSON 1 PART 2

My Time

My Score

Now let's try some more. Work out the questions on some scrap paper and then mark your answers on the answer sheet. You have 10 minutes to complete this task. Write the time you took and your score in the boxes above once you've finished. Again, remember that an adult needs to mark these for you.

1 Rugby Team A scored 23 points and Rugby Team B 56 points. By how many points did Rugby Team B win?

2 The temperature in Oslo was 7°C during the day and fell 17°C during the night. What was the temperature at night?

3 If a charity raffle raised £433 one year and £716 the next, how much more money was raised in the second year?

4 If a company recycled 22,039 cans in April and 20,145 in May, how many fewer cans were recycled in May than in April?

5 Looking at the table below, how many more children attended school on Tuesday than on Thursday?

Day	Monday	Tuesday	Wednesday	Thursday	Friday
Number of children	342	603	751	289	419

6 A library had 21,068 books in January and had 22,128 books in December. How many more books did it have in December?

7 The population of Goodchester is 2,189,053 and the population of Greatfield is 1,809,652. How many fewer people live in Greatfield than Goodchester?

8 Vincent cycled 137 miles. How much further did he travel than Guy, who cycled 49 miles?

9 A bowl contains 3 litres of water. How many fewer millilitres of water did it contain when it held 2 litres 340ml?

10 How much taller is a building measuring 1,034ft than one measuring 988ft?

LESSON 1 PART 2: ANSWER SHEET

Mark your answer by putting a horizontal line in 1 of the boxes, as in the example below.

Example:

```
383 ☐
217 ▬
723 ☐
223 ☐
287 ☐
```

1
- 78 ☐
- 33 ☐
- 18 ☐
- 32 ☐
- 34 ☐

2
- 24°C ☐
- 10°C ☐
- –10°C ☐
- –24°C ☐
- –7°C ☐

3
- £323 ☐
- £1,149 ☐
- £616 ☐
- £383 ☐
- £283 ☐

4
- 42,184 ☐
- 1,894 ☐
- 2,114 ☐
- 1,914 ☐
- 1,194 ☐

5
- 53 ☐
- 314 ☐
- 462 ☐
- 130 ☐
- 486 ☐

6
- 1,140 ☐
- 1,160 ☐
- 1,940 ☐
- 43,196 ☐
- 1,060 ☐

7
- 3,998,705 ☐
- 1,780,601 ☐
- 380,601 ☐
- 381,401 ☐
- 379,401 ☐

8
- 186 miles ☐
- 112 miles ☐
- 92 miles ☐
- 88 miles ☐
- 108 miles ☐

9
- 134ml ☐
- 234ml ☐
- 660ml ☐
- 3,000ml ☐
- 5,340ml ☐

10
- 154ft ☐
- 46ft ☐
- 2,022ft ☐
- 8,854ft ☐
- 154ft ☐

LESSON 2 Calculating Fractions of a Whole Number

In this exercise, you'll be given an amount and asked to calculate a fraction or part of this. To do this you need to learn the following method: to find the fraction of a whole number, divide the total amount by the denominator. Then multiply the answer by the numerator. Let's look at an example.

Example

A local shop's car park can hold 36 cars.
If it's $\frac{5}{9}$ full, how many cars are parked there?

The possible answers are:

14

 4

31

27

20

So as explained above,

First divide the total by the denominator of the fraction: $36 \div 9 = 4$

Then multiply your answer by the numerator: $4 \times 5 = 20$

So there are 20 cars in the car park.

HELPFUL HINT

Make sure you don't simply work out 1 part of the answer. In the question above it asks for five-ninths of the total not just one-ninth. The answer for one-ninth is there in the answer choices to catch you out, so watch out for these.

LESSON 2 PART 1

My Time

My Score

Now look at the questions below. Work out the answers on some scrap paper and then mark them on the answer sheet. You have 10 minutes to complete this task. Write the time you took in the box above once you've finished. Remember to get an adult to mark your answers. Then write your score in the box at the top of this page.

1. In an ice cream shop, 96 ice creams have been sold, of which ¼ are vanilla. How many vanilla ice creams have been sold?

2. In a school of 16 classes ⅜ go on a trip to the zoo. How many classes stay at school?

3. A factory makes 490 cars each week. Of these ⅐ are blue, 4/7 are red and the rest are green. How many green cars are made each week?

4. In an art gallery with 64 paintings, ⅛ are oil. How many oil paintings are in the gallery?

5. A pizza parlour sells 120 pizzas. Of these, ⅕ were pepperoni and 3/10 were vegetarian. How many pepperoni were sold?

6. Of the 270 people on a ship, 2/9 are members of the crew. How many passengers are there?

7. A hardware store has sold 144 items. Of these ⅙ are shovels, ¼ are nails and the rest are hammers. How many hammers have been sold?

8. If 3/7 of a sack of 84 letters are first class, and the rest are second class, how many are second class?

9. In a box of 360 vegetables, 2/9 are rotten. How many is this?

10. In a year of 52 children, 5/13 play netball. How many children in the year would this be?

LESSON 2 PART 1: ANSWER SHEET

Mark your answer by putting a horizontal line in 1 of the boxes, as in the example below.

Example:

```
14 ☐
 4 ☐
31 ☐
27 ☐
20 ▬
```

1
```
 92 ☐
 72 ☐
 24 ☐
100 ☐
 25 ☐
```

2
```
24 ☐
 8 ☐
13 ☐
10 ☐
 6 ☐
```

3
```
245 ☐
 70 ☐
140 ☐
 14 ☐
420 ☐
```

4
```
 8 ☐
64 ☐
72 ☐
56 ☐
 9 ☐
```

5
```
12 ☐
 6 ☐
18 ☐
24 ☐
30 ☐
```

6
```
210 ☐
 63 ☐
207 ☐
 30 ☐
 93 ☐
```

7
```
132 ☐
 84 ☐
 12 ☐
 60 ☐
 19 ☐
```

8
```
28 ☐
48 ☐
21 ☐
12 ☐
11 ☐
```

9
```
180 ☐
 18 ☐
 40 ☐
 80 ☐
280 ☐
```

10
```
65 ☐
18 ☐
34 ☐
 4 ☐
20 ☐
```

How Did You Do? Let's Find Out!

Remember, there is no self-marking in this book. Please get an adult to mark your answers.

If you scored 8 or more out of 10

These questions can be quite tricky so this is a good score. If you didn't get them all right, check where you went wrong. This will help you score higher on the next set of questions.

If you scored fewer than 8 out of 10

You should aim to score higher in the next set of questions. Check the questions you got wrong and make sure you understand how to apply the method before you move on.

HELPFUL HINT

Do you remember which number is called the denominator and which is the numerator? If you don't, remind yourself before moving on.

TIPS FOR SPEEDING UP

Use your knowledge of multiplication facts (times tables) to help you. You'll be able to notice relationships between numbers very quickly if you know these thoroughly.

LESSON 2 PART 2

My Time

My Score

Now let's try some more. Work out the questions on some scrap paper and then mark your answers on the answer sheet. I will only give you 10 minutes to complete this task. Write the time you took and your score in the boxes above once you've finished. Again, remember that an adult needs to mark your test for you.

1. In a book of 280 pages $\frac{1}{20}$ have illustrations. How many pages is this?

2. Out of an audience of 320 people, 80 are children. What fraction of the audience does this represent?

3. A factory makes 660 sweets and $\frac{2}{11}$ of these are not suitable to sell. How many are ready to sell?

4. In a zoo of 168 animals, $\frac{1}{4}$ are mammals, $\frac{5}{8}$ are birds and the rest are reptiles. How many reptiles are there in the zoo?

5. In a clothing store, of 2,088 clothes $\frac{3}{4}$ are coats and $\frac{2}{8}$ are trousers. How many trousers are there?

6. A doctor sees 36 patients in a day. Of these $\frac{5}{9}$ require medicine. How many do not require medicine?

7. In a race with 35 competitors, $\frac{2}{5}$ fell over a hurdle. How many was this?

8. In a spelling test Joel got $\frac{5}{6}$ of the 24 words correct. How many words did he get incorrect?

9. In the month of April it rained for a third of the days. How many days did it not rain?

10. Carly watches two-thirds of a television programme. If the programme was 45 minutes long, how many minutes did she see?

LESSON 2 PART 2: ANSWER SHEET

Mark your answer by putting a horizontal line in 1 of the boxes, as in the example below.

Example:

```
14 ☐
 4 ☐
31 ☐
27 ☐
20 ▬
```

1
```
 20 ☐
 14 ☐
 28 ☐
260 ☐
  8 ☐
```

2
```
½ ☐
⅓ ☐
¼ ☐
⅕ ☐
⅙ ☐
```

3
```
 99 ☐
 60 ☐
540 ☐
559 ☐
594 ☐
```

4
```
20 ☐
21 ☐
22 ☐
23 ☐
24 ☐
```

5
```
1,044 ☐
  130 ☐
  131 ☐
  261 ☐
  522 ☐
```

6
```
 4 ☐
 9 ☐
13 ☐
16 ☐
18 ☐
```

7
```
 7 ☐
10 ☐
14 ☐
17 ☐
25 ☐
```

8
```
 4 ☐
 6 ☐
 7 ☐
10 ☐
18 ☐
```

9
```
 6 ☐
10 ☐
15 ☐
20 ☐
24 ☐
```

10
```
15 minutes ☐
20 minutes ☐
25 minutes ☐
30 minutes ☐
    1 hour ☐
```

LESSON 3 Finding the Whole Number from a Fraction

In this exercise, you'll need to calculate the answer by using the opposite method to the one you used in lesson 2. You'll be dividing the number you've been given by the numerator and then multiplying the answer by the denominator.

Be careful here as it's easy to confuse these questions with the ones you've just tackled in lesson 2. It's best to always read the question twice to ensure that you've understood what needs to be done. Let's look at an example: I'm going to use the same example as lesson 2 to show you the difference.

Example 1

In a car park $5/9$ of the spaces are full. If 20 spaces are full, how many parking spaces does the car park have in total?

You know that 20 spaces are filled and that $20 = 5/9$ so you need to find $1/9$ first.

You do this by dividing 20 by the numerator: $20 \div 5 = 4$

If $4 = 1/9$ then to find the total you must multiply 4 by $9 = 36$.

So the car park has <u>36</u> spaces in total.

HELPFUL HINT

Remember, if you start dividing and find your answer is not going to be a whole number, check again to make sure you're using the correct method.

Example 2

Joely calculates that she spent £4.50 in a shop which was $5/7$ of her money. How much money did she take to the shop originally?

For the example above you know that £4.50 is $5/7$ of Joely's total money. You have to find $1/7$ and you do this by dividing £4.50 by 5 which gives us 90p. Then you multiply this amount by 7 to find her original amount of money which is <u>£6.30</u> and that's the answer you mark on your answer grid.

LESSON 3 PART 1

Now look at the questions below. Work out the answers on some scrap paper and then mark them on the answer sheet. Again, you have only 10 minutes to complete this task. Write the time you took in the box above once you've finished. Remember to get an adult to mark your answers. Then write your score in the box at the top of this page.

1 In a dance class, 12 people, that is one-fifth, prefer hip hop. How many people are in the class?

2 If 3cm of snow fell 1 night and this was $1/7$ of the total, how much fell altogether?

3 If 16 children took part in a gymnastics competition and this was $2/9$ of the year group, how many children were in the year group?

4 Paul read 73 pages, which was a third of his book. How many pages does the book have in total?

5 If a fish tank holds 8 litres of water when it is $2/5$ full, how many more litres would you need to fill it completely?

6 If an aeroplane has reached three-quarters of its highest altitude at 24,000ft, what is the highest it can fly?

7 A hill walker has travelled $3/11$ of the walk after 9 miles. How long is the complete walk?

8 Adam has £648 in his bank account, which represents $8/9$ of his total savings. How much money does he have in total?

9 If a campsite is seven-tenths full when it has 56 tents pitched on its site, how many more tents can be pitched before it is completely full?

10 If a container holds 200ml when it is $1/6$ full, how much can it hold in total?

LESSON 3 PART 1: ANSWER SHEET

Mark your answer by putting a horizontal line in 1 of the boxes, as in the examples below.

Example 1:

```
14  ☐
45  ☐
36  ▬
34  ☐
29  ☐
```

Example 2:

```
£4.15   ☐
£0.90   ☐
£6.30   ▬
£22.50  ☐
£3.50   ☐
```

1
```
7   ☐
17  ☐
18  ☐
52  ☐
60  ☐
```

2
```
10cm  ☐
11cm  ☐
21cm  ☐
22cm  ☐
28cm  ☐
```

3
```
8   ☐
14  ☐
18  ☐
25  ☐
72  ☐
```

4
```
70   ☐
76   ☐
219  ☐
213  ☐
216  ☐
```

5
```
40 litres  ☐
12 litres  ☐
16 litres  ☐
15 litres  ☐
10 litres  ☐
```

6
```
32,000ft  ☐
72,000ft  ☐
12,000ft  ☐
8,000ft   ☐
6,000ft   ☐
```

7
```
14 miles  ☐
27 miles  ☐
99 miles  ☐
33 miles  ☐
23 miles  ☐
```

8
```
£72   ☐
£81   ☐
£729  ☐
£576  ☐
£631  ☐
```

9
```
73  ☐
80  ☐
42  ☐
24  ☐
70  ☐
```

10
```
0.2 litres    ☐
1,200 litres  ☐
1.2 litres    ☐
12 litres     ☐
120 litres    ☐
```

How Did You Do? Let's Find Out!

Remember, there is no self-marking in this book. Please get an adult to mark your answers.

If you scored 8 or more out of 10

This is a good score, well done. If you got 8 or 9, check where you went wrong before you move on to the next set of questions.

If you scored fewer than 8 out of 10

You should try to aim for a higher score for the next set of questions. Check the questions you got wrong and make sure you understand how to apply the method before you move on.

TIPS FOR SPEEDING UP

Use your knowledge of multiplication facts (times tables) to help you. You'll be able to notice relationships between numbers very quickly if you know these thoroughly.

LESSON 3 PART 2

My Time

My Score

Now let's try some more. Work out the questions on some scrap paper and then mark your answers on the answer sheet. As usual you have 10 minutes to complete this task. Write the time you took and your score in the boxes above once you've finished. Again, remember that an adult needs to mark your test for you.

1. A marina is $4/7$ full when it contains 44 yachts. How many can it hold when full?

2. Bobby calculates that after climbing 72 steps of a building he is $3/4$ of the way up. How many more steps are there to the top?

3. A kitchen cupboard holds 507 tins of food when $3/8$ full. How many can it hold when completely full?

4. A website has 12 pages and it is $4/5$ complete. How many pages will it have when it is finished?

5. A restaurant seats 42 people when it is $6/7$ full. How many people can it seat when completely full?

6. If a computer shop has sold 35 computers and these represent $5/7$ of its stock, how many remain to be sold?

7. If Damon is 12 years old, which is a quarter of his father's age, how old is his father?

8. If a bookshelf can hold 16 books when it is $2/7$ full, how many books can fit on it in total?

9. A van is making a round of deliveries. After 18 deliveries, it is three-fifths of the way through its round. How many more deliveries does it need to make?

10. A pizza which has been cooking for 20 minutes is two-thirds through its cooking time. How long should it be cooked for in total?

LESSON 3 PART 2: ANSWER SHEET

Mark your answer by putting a horizontal line in 1 of the boxes, as in the examples below.

Example 1:

14	☐
45	☐
36	▬
34	☐
29	☐

Example 2:

£4.15	☐
£0.90	☐
£6.30	▬
£22.50	☐
£3.50	☐

1
40	☐
44	☐
48	☐
77	☐
88	☐

2
24	☐
42	☐
96	☐
54	☐
72	☐

3
1,521	☐
4,056	☐
1,352	☐
1,376	☐
1,328	☐

4
15	☐
20	☐
9	☐
48	☐
60	☐

5
36	☐
49	☐
35	☐
55	☐
56	☐

6
49	☐
40	☐
42	☐
14	☐
41	☐

7
16	☐
29	☐
48	☐
36	☐
60	☐

8
56	☐
28	☐
14	☐
23	☐
32	☐

9
54	☐
12	☐
21	☐
23	☐
30	☐

10
40 minutes	☐
45 minutes	☐
35 minutes	☐
30 minutes	☐
25 minutes	☐

LESSON 4 Simplifying Fractions

In this exercise, you'll need to work out what the fraction is in its raw form, then simplify it to find the answer given on the grid.

To simplify a fraction make a list of the factors of both the numerator and the denominator, then check to see which one or more factors appear in both lists. Choose the biggest of these and divide both parts of your fraction by it to get the fraction in its simplest form. Let's look at an example.

Example 1

Hannibal has completed 15 laps of a 25-lap race.
Show this fraction in its lowest terms.

$\frac{15}{25}$ factors: 1, 3, 5, 15
factors: 1, 5, 25

So you divide the numerator and denominator by 5 since this is the greatest common factor.

$\frac{15 \div 5}{25 \div 5} = \frac{3}{5}$

So your fraction in its simplest form is $\frac{3}{5}$.

TIP FOR SPEEDING UP

Use your knowledge of multiplication facts to find the greatest common factor quickly in your head instead of writing all the factors down – this will save you valuable time.

Example 2

Cody left out 4 questions on a test of a possible 36.
Show this information as a fraction in its simplest form.

For the question above, you would use your knowledge of multiplication facts to save time. Looking at the number 4 you can see that its factors are 1, 2 and 4. You take the largest of these and see if it divides into 36, which it does.

Now divide 4 and 36 by 4, which gives you 1 and 9. Your answer must be a fraction, which in this case is $\frac{1}{9}$ so that's the answer you mark on the answer grid.

LESSON 4 PART 1

My Time

My Score

Now look at the questions below. Work out the answers on some scrap paper and then mark them on the answer sheet. Mark your time in the box provided once you've finished. Remember to get an adult to mark your answers. Then write your score in the box at the top of this page.

You have 10 minutes to complete these, so work quickly.

1 In a pet shop of 36 animals, 12 are cats. Show this information as a fraction in its lowest terms.

2 Ally has read 42 pages of her 210-page book. What fraction is this in its simplest form?

3 In a restaurant, 13 of the 52 seats are empty; what fraction is this in its simplest form?

4 A football team won 21 matches, drew 11 and lost 7. What fraction of its matches did it win?

5 Freddie spent 12 days in June on holiday. Give this as a fraction in its lowest terms.

6 If 24 children of a class of 32 remembered their swimming kit, what fraction forgot theirs? Give this fraction in its lowest terms.

7 At a carboot sale, Chris sold 60 of his 105 items. What fraction remained unsold? Give this fraction in its lowest terms.

8 A postal delivery service was able deliver all but 3 of its 84 parcels one day. What fraction did it deliver? Give this fraction in its lowest terms.

9 In a sale a store sold 120 of its 480 items at half price. Give this fraction in its simplest form.

10 If Alvin has used 108 of his free 300 minutes on his phone, what fraction remains for him to use? Give this fraction in its lowest terms.

LESSON 4 PART 1: ANSWER SHEET

Mark your answer by putting a horizontal line in 1 of the boxes, as in the examples below.

Example 1:

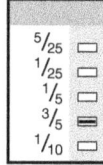

Example 2:

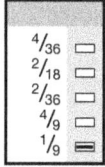

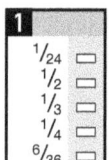 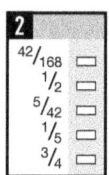 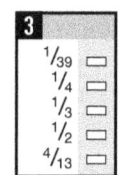 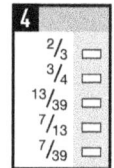

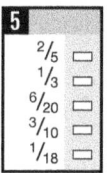  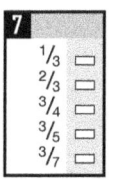 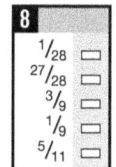

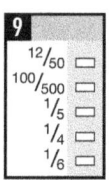 

How Did You Do? Let's Find Out!

Remember, there is no self-marking in this book. Please get an adult to mark your answers.

If you scored 8 or more out of 10

These questions can be quite tricky so this is a good score. Check where you went wrong and look at the tips for speeding up below before you move on to the next set of questions.

If you scored fewer than 8 out of 10

These are tricky questions but try to score higher in the next set of questions. Check the questions you got wrong and make sure you understand how to apply the method.

HELPFUL HINT

- Did you remember the method? Did you remember to simplify your answers? Have another look to understand where you went wrong.

TIPS FOR SPEEDING UP

- Use your knowledge of multiplication facts (times tables) to help you. You'll be able to notice relationships between numbers very quickly if you know these thoroughly. You may have noticed this is becoming a common theme – so learn them!

- If you've got big numbers for the denominator and numerator, look to divide by 10 or halve them first to get them down to more manageable numbers. This way, you'll find it easier to simplify them further without spending too much time on it.

LESSON 4 PART 2

My Time

My Score

Now look at the questions below. Work them out on some scrap paper and then mark your answers on the answer sheet. Mark your time and your score in the boxes provided once you've finished and get an adult to mark your answers.

You have 10 minutes to complete these, so work quickly.

1. There are currants in 120 out of 150 buns in a baker's shop. What is this as a fraction in its simplest form?

2. Saleh runs a marathon of 26 miles. When he is 13 miles through the race what fraction has he run? Give this as a fraction in its lowest terms.

3. A pizza is split into 18 equal pieces, of which 6 pieces are pepperoni and the rest are chicken. What fraction of the pizza is chicken? Give this as a fraction in its lowest terms.

4. An aeroplane has flown 2,300 miles of its 6,900-mile journey. What fraction remains for it to travel? Give this as a fraction in its lowest terms.

5. Ronda calculates that she has completed 14 of her 26 pieces of holiday homework. What fraction is this in its simplest form?

6. Ron notices that 7 pages of his 49-page magazine have advertisements. What fraction is this? Give this as a fraction in its lowest terms.

7. Karen has used 12 out of her 16 cups. What fraction of cups remain unused? Give this as a fraction in its lowest terms.

8. A factory makes 4,200 pencils each week. Of these, 120 are green. What fraction is this in its lowest terms?

9. Oliver calculates that he needs to save £7.50 to buy a new toy train. If he has saved £1.50 already, what fraction remains for him to save? Give this as a fraction in its lowest terms.

10. In a school week there are 30 periods of lessons. If 14 of these are spent on teaching sciences, what fraction is this in its simplest form?

LESSON 4 PART 2: ANSWER SHEET

Mark your answer by putting a horizontal line in 1 of the boxes, as in the examples below.

Example 1:

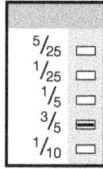

Example 2:

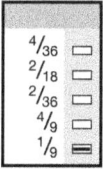

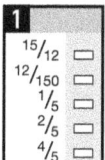

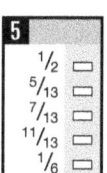

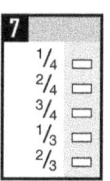
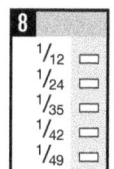

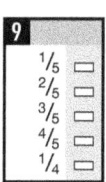

LESSON 5 Rounding Numbers and Decimals

In this exercise, you'll need to identify the number which needs rounding and then round it correctly.

Rounding is when you don't use the exact number and instead you use the closest whole number.

Think of it this way, if you had £4.97 in your pocket and someone asked you how much money you had, you might well tell them that you had £5. It's not exact but it's a lot quicker and easier than counting the money and telling them the exact amount.

To begin you check the question to see what decimal place the number or decimal is to be rounded to. Next underline the digit to the right of this place value and check how this digit can be rounded.

If the digit on the right is 0, 1, 2, 3 or 4, the rounded digit remains the same value; if the digit on the right is 5, 6, 7, 8, or 9, the rounded digit increases by 1.

When you've finished rounding, all the digits including and after the underlined one will become 0.

Let's look at some examples.

Example 1

Round 1,293 to the nearest hundred.

In this number the 2 is in the hundreds column so you underline the digit on its right.

    1,2<u>9</u>3   You know that 9 rounds up by adding 1 to the digit on its left, so your new number is 1,3<u>9</u>3.

Next, all the digits including and after the underlined digit become 0 so 1,3<u>9</u>3 becomes 1,300.

Your final answer is <u>1,300</u>.

Example 2

Round 37.13 to the nearest tenth.

In this case you need to be careful, because the question says <u>tenth</u> not <u>ten</u>. So you must underline the digit 2 places after the decimal point.

    37.1<u>3</u>   The digit on the right of the number after the decimal point is 3 so the rounded digit keeps its value. You then change the underlined digit to 0.

    37.1<u>0</u> is the answer.

LESSON 5 PART 1

My Time

My Score

Now look at the questions below. Work out your answers and then mark your answers on the corresponding answer grids. Mark your time in the box provided once you've finished. Remember to get an adult to mark your answers. Then write your score in the box at the top of this page.

You have 10 minutes to complete these, so work quickly.

1. The population of Funchester is 2,167,413. What is this population to the nearest hundred thousand?

2. Barak has £3.99 in his wallet. How much money does he have to the nearest pound?

3. If there are 852 students in a school, how many are there to the nearest hundred?

4. A skier records a race time of 1 minute 23.67 seconds. What is his time to the nearest tenth of a second?

5. A lamp post is measured at 5.32m. What height is it to the nearest 10cm?

6. A bottle contains 581ml of water. What is this amount to the nearest 100ml?

7. A local business collected 24,568 empty cans for recycling. What is this number to the nearest thousand?

8. A flower measures 234.761mm. How tall is it to the closest hundredth of 1mm?

9. A book contains 1,209 pages. What is this rounded to the nearest hundred pages?

10. A factory produced 12,056 cars in a month. What is this number to the nearest 10 thousand?

LESSON 5 PART 1: ANSWER SHEET

Mark your answer by putting a horizontal line in 1 of the boxes, as in the examples below.

Example 1:

- 1,200 ☐
- 1,300 ▬
- 2,000 ☐
- 1,290 ☐
- 1,000 ☐

Example 2:

- 37.10 ▬
- 37.00 ☐
- 37.20 ☐
- 38.00 ☐
- 37.30 ☐

1
- 2,100,000 ☐
- 2,200,000 ☐
- 2,170,000 ☐
- 2,167,000 ☐
- 2,000,000 ☐

2
- £3.00 ☐
- £3.90 ☐
- £4.00 ☐
- £4.90 ☐
- £0.90 ☐

3
- 900 ☐
- 800 ☐
- 850 ☐
- 950 ☐
- 860 ☐

4
- 1m 23.6s ☐
- 1m 23.7s ☐
- 1m 24.00s ☐
- 1m 23.60s ☐
- 1m 24.6s ☐

5
- 5.00m ☐
- 5.02m ☐
- 5.30m ☐
- 5.40m ☐
- 5.50m ☐

6
- 500ml ☐
- 800ml ☐
- 100ml ☐
- 600ml ☐
- 700ml ☐

7
- 20,000 ☐
- 24,000 ☐
- 25,000 ☐
- 22,000 ☐
- 23,000 ☐

8
- 234.6mm ☐
- 234.7mm ☐
- 234.8mm ☐
- 234.76mm ☐
- 234.77mm ☐

9
- 1,100 ☐
- 1,200 ☐
- 1,300 ☐
- 1,400 ☐
- 1,500 ☐

10
- 10,000 ☐
- 11,000 ☐
- 12,000 ☐
- 13,000 ☐
- 14,000 ☐

How Did You Do? Let's Find Out!

Remember, there is no self-marking in this book. Please get an adult to mark your answers.

If you scored 8 or more out of 10

These types of question should be easy enough, provided you read the instructions carefully. There are several ways to ask questions about rounding so be wary.

If you got 8 or 9 try to improve on the next set of questions by checking where you went wrong, and look at the further hints below before you move on.

If you scored fewer than 8 out of 10

These types of question are quite straightforward so let's work to improve your score. Check the questions you got wrong and make sure you understand which number needed rounding. Then look at the further hints below before you move on to the next set of questions.

Further hints

⇨ A common mistake students make when rounding would be in a number such as 173. If you're told to round this number to the nearest 10, you may think it should be 180. This is wrong since the digit directly on the right of the 7 is only 3. The correct answer is 170. Some students round up 7 because the 7 is a high number. Don't make this mistake – remember it's the digit directly on the right which lets you know which way to round.

⇨ Sometimes you might get a question where you round one place value column but it means you need to round another too. Let's look at an example.

Example

Round the number 2,398 to the nearest 10.

This question looks straightforward enough but watch what happens when you round the tens.

2,39<u>8</u>   here you can see that the 9 should round up to become 10. But you can't write 10 in a column so you write 0 and round the 3 up by 1. It's just like when you add and you have too many for a place value column – you carry the amount over to the next place value column if it fills up. Finally, make sure the underlined digit becomes 0.

So your final answer would be 2,400 even though you are rounding to the tens. And strangely enough, if you were told to round this number to the nearest hundred, the answer would be exactly the same!

Watch out for these – they might be included in the next 10 questions.

LESSON 5 PART 2

My Time

My Score

Now let's try some more. Work out the answers and then mark them on the corresponding answer grids. Write the time you took and your score in the boxes above once you've finished. Again, remember that an adult needs to mark your test for you.

You have 10 minutes to complete these, so work quickly.

1. Mr Biggs wins £2,351 on the lottery. How much did he win rounded to the nearest thousand pounds?

2. A store sold 23,973 shoes in a week. How many is this to the nearest hundred?

3. If 34,029 people attended a football match, how many were there to the nearest thousand?

4. Alfred ran the 100m race in 9.009 seconds. What was his time to the nearest tenth of a second?

5. A town was 37.08 miles away. How far is this to the nearest mile?

6. A postal worker delivered 8,372 letters in 1 week. How many letters is this to the nearest hundred?

7. An aeroplane travels 23,643 miles. What is this number to the nearest 10 thousand?

8. An internet search engine produces 31,408,296 results. What is this to the nearest million?

9. A telephone directory contains 45,273 numbers. What is this rounded to the nearest 10 thousand?

10. A snail crawled 27.835mm in an hour. How far is this rounded to the nearest hundredth of a millimetre?

LESSON 5 PART 2: ANSWER SHEET

Mark your answer by putting a horizontal line in 1 of the boxes, as in the examples below.

Example 1:

- 1,200 ☐
- 1,300 ▬
- 2,000 ☐
- 1,290 ☐
- 1,000 ☐

Example 2:

- 37.10 ▬
- 37.00 ☐
- 37.20 ☐
- 38.00 ☐
- 37.30 ☐

1
- £2,000 ☐
- £2,100 ☐
- £3,000 ☐
- £2,400 ☐
- £2,300 ☐

2
- 23,900 ☐
- 24,000 ☐
- 23,700 ☐
- 24,900 ☐
- 24,700 ☐

3
- 30,000 ☐
- 35,000 ☐
- 34,000 ☐
- 34,020 ☐
- 33,020 ☐

4
- 9.0s ☐
- 9.001s ☐
- 9.01s ☐
- 9.1s ☐
- 0.91s ☐

5
- 38 miles ☐
- 38.1 miles ☐
- 37.1 miles ☐
- 37 miles ☐
- 36 miles ☐

6
- 8,000 ☐
- 8,300 ☐
- 8,400 ☐
- 8,370 ☐
- 8,380 ☐

7
- 20,000 ☐
- 23,000 ☐
- 22,000 ☐
- 21,000 ☐
- 24,000 ☐

8
- 30 million ☐
- 31 million ☐
- 32 million ☐
- 33 million ☐
- 34 million ☐

9
- 46,000 ☐
- 47,000 ☐
- 48,000 ☐
- 49,000 ☐
- 50,000 ☐

10
- 28mm ☐
- 27mm ☐
- 27.8mm ☐
- 27.83mm ☐
- 27.84mm ☐

LESSON 6 Turning Fractions into Decimals and Percentages

In this exercise, you'll need to think of the link between percentages, fractions and decimals. Often in these questions, a fraction is given and you're asked to convert it into a percentage. Remember that you can use your factors of 100 to help with a lot of these.

Let's look at an example.

Example 1

If a pizza delivery service has delivered 39 out of 50 pizzas, what percentage has it delivered?

First set the numbers out as a fraction then work out what to multiply the denominator by to make 100. In this case it's 2. Make sure you multiply the numerator by the same amount.

$$\frac{39}{50} \times \frac{2}{2} = \frac{78}{100}$$

Then: 78 out of 100 is <u>78%</u>.

You can go one step further and also turn this into a decimal. All you have to do is look at your new fraction which is 78 one-hundredths and place that on a place value chart.

units	decimal point	tenths	hundredths
0	.	7	8

So written as a decimal it would be <u>0.78</u>

Example 2

A pop star receives fan mail every day. If she has replied to 43 out 50 letters, what percentage has she not yet replied to?

You would answer the question above by using your knowledge of the factors of 100.

First read the question carefully and notice that you need to work out how many letters she has not replied to. This is 7 out of 50. You know that 50 x 2 = 100 so you then do the same to 7 which gives you 14. So <u>14%</u> is the answer you mark on the answer grid.

LESSON 6 PART 1

My Time

My Score

Now look at the questions below. Work out the answers on some scrap paper and then mark them on the answer sheet opposite. Write the time you took in the box above once you've finished. Remember to get an adult to mark your answers. Then write your score in the box at the top of this page.

You have 10 minutes to complete these, so work quickly.

1 Bronwyn calculates that she has $^{31}/_{100}$ of a one pound coin in her pocket. What amount is this?

2 Herman took a driving test. He performed 16 of the 20 required manoeuvres correctly. What percentage is this?

3 Andrea and her 4 friends order pizza for dinner. It is split into 10 segments and they each eat 2. What percentage does each eat?

4 Haley has read 110 pages of a 440-page book. What percentage of the book remains for her to read?

5 If a theatre holds 300 people and 240 seats are taken, what percentage of the seats are still empty?

6 The local swimming pool can hold 1,000 cubic litres of water. If it currently contains 400 cubic litres, what percentage is this?

7 A choir comprises 50 people. If 21 of them are female, what percentage is male?

8 If a car holds 13 litres of petrol when it is 20% full, how much can it hold when completely full?

9 Fifi has been growing sunflowers. If 23 out of 25 seeds grew, what percentage failed to grow?

10 If 60% of a school year gets grade 'B' in their exams and this represents 48 students, how many students are there in the year?

LESSON 6 PART 1: ANSWER SHEET

Mark your answer by putting a horizontal line in 1 of the boxes, as in the examples below.

Example 1:

```
39% ☐
50% ☐
89% ☐
78% ▬
11% ☐
```

Example 2:

```
 7% ☐
14% ▬
43% ☐
50% ☐
86% ☐
```

1
```
£3.10  ☐
£31.00 ☐
£0.31  ☐
£3.01  ☐
£0.03  ☐
```

2
```
 4% ☐
36% ☐
16% ☐
80% ☐
20% ☐
```

3
```
 2% ☐
10% ☐
20% ☐
12% ☐
22% ☐
```

4
```
330% ☐
 33% ☐
 55% ☐
 44% ☐
 75% ☐
```

5
```
20% ☐
40% ☐
60% ☐
80% ☐
95% ☐
```

6
```
  4% ☐
400% ☐
 40% ☐
 60% ☐
 80% ☐
```

7
```
21% ☐
29% ☐
42% ☐
58% ☐
71% ☐
```

8
```
 7 litres ☐
20 litres ☐
33 litres ☐
53 litres ☐
65 litres ☐
```

9
```
 2% ☐
48% ☐
 8% ☐
92% ☐
10% ☐
```

10
```
108 ☐
 12 ☐
 60 ☐
 80 ☐
100 ☐
```

How Did You Do? Let's Find Out!

Remember, there is no self-marking in this book. Please get an adult to mark your answers.

If you scored 8 or more out of 10

This is a good score, but if you scored 8 or 9 try to improve on the next set of questions by checking where you went wrong. Look at the further hints below and tips for speeding up on the next page before you move on.

If you scored fewer than 8 out of 10

To improve this score check the questions you got wrong and make sure you understand how to apply the method. Read the further hints below and tips for speeding up on the next page.

Further hints

⇨ Do you understand what to do? If not, get an adult to read the instructions and examples with you. Then have a look at any questions you got wrong and make sure you understand why.

⇨ Did you notice in questions 8 and 10 that I reversed the process? Watch out for these and if you're unsure about them, go back to lesson 6 in the first maths book in the series (*Practise & Pass 11+ Level One: Discover Maths*) and take another look at the method.

⇨ Did you notice that questions 4, 5 and 6 were not factors of 100? Remember to simplify these fractions first then multiply them up to find a percentage. If you're still unsure go back to lesson 6 in the first maths book in the series and take another look at the method.

TIPS FOR SPEEDING UP

- Know your factors of 100 off by heart – this will save you valuable time.

- Practise multiplying 2 digit numbers quickly using your multiplication facts to help you.

- Look at your multiple choice answer sheet to help you eliminate any obviously incorrect answers. For example, if a question asks you to calculate 12 out of 20 as a percentage, you could immediately ignore any answers which are lower than 50%. This is because 12 is more than half of 20 and half of a number is 50%.

- Use your multiplication facts to help you simplify larger numbers quickly. Then you'll be able to calculate the percentage more quickly. For example, if you were asked to work out 120 out of 200 as a percentage you could simplify this by dividing both numbers by 10. This would leave you with 12 out of 20, which are easier numbers to work with.

LESSON 6 PART 2

Now let's try some more. Work out the answers on some scrap paper and then mark your answers on the opposite page. Watch out for those fractions you need to simplify. Write the time you took and your score in the boxes above once you've finished. Again, remember that an adult needs to mark these for you.

You have 10 minutes to complete these, so work quickly.

1. Fahad scored 95% on a spelling test. If the test was out of 20, how many questions did he get correct?

2. If 43 out of 50 trains arrived at a station on time, what percentage of the trains did not arrive on time?

3. Clive calculates that he lives exactly 1,000m from his nearest shop. Once he has walked 75% of the way, how much further must he walk to reach the shop?

4. Antoine notices that when the car park he manages is 40% full it holds 80 cars. How many cars can it hold when completely full?

5. A local restaurant serves 63 out of a possible 90 customers one night. What percentage is this?

6. In a local talent completion, 73,000 out of a possible 100,000 people voted for Hannibal. What percentage is this?

7. In a cinema, when 23 seats are full this represents 1%. How many people can the cinema hold when it is completely full?

8. If 70 students of a school's 200 students are going on a residential trip, what percentage is staying behind?

9. Six twenty-fourths of cars in a garage require an oil change. What is this written as a percentage?

10. Some students have been collecting cans for recycling. If they collected 860 cans and 215 cannot be recycled, what percentage can be recycled?

LESSON 6 PART 2: ANSWER SHEET

Mark your answer by putting a horizontal line in 1 of the boxes, as in the examples below.

Example 1:

39%	☐
50%	☐
89%	☐
78%	▬
11%	☐

Example 2:

7%	☐
14%	▬
43%	☐
50%	☐
86%	☐

1
75	☐
19	☐
18	☐
17	☐
16	☐

2
7%	☐
14%	☐
43%	☐
50%	☐
93%	☐

3
25km	☐
0.25km	☐
2.5km	☐
0.75km	☐
7.5km	☐

4
40	☐
80	☐
120	☐
160	☐
200	☐

5
17%	☐
63%	☐
70%	☐
87%	☐
90%	☐

6
17%	☐
70%	☐
73%	☐
80%	☐
90%	☐

7
23	☐
24	☐
230	☐
2,300	☐
2,400	☐

8
130%	☐
35%	☐
70%	☐
65%	☐
60%	☐

9
18%	☐
24%	☐
30%	☐
36%	☐
25%	☐

10
20%	☐
25%	☐
30%	☐
50%	☐
75%	☐

LESSON 7 Calculating Probability

In this exercise, you'll need to calculate how likely an outcome is, which is also called the probability of an outcome.

Probability is how likely something is to happen.

To do this you need to work out all the possible outcomes and all the favourable outcomes. Then you set these out as a fraction. The number of possible outcomes becomes the denominator and the number of favourable outcomes becomes the numerator. Let's look at an example.

Example

Colin's teacher has boxes of coloured pencils. In each box there are 3 blue, 5 red and 2 yellow pencils. Colin picks out a pencil at random. What is the probability that it will be a yellow pencil?

First you work out the number of possible outcomes, which is 10 since there are 10 pencils in total – this is your denominator.

Then you put 2 as your numerator as there are 2 yellow pencils. The answer is $^2/_{10}$ which you must simplify to $^1/_5$.

HELPFUL HINTS

- Remember that probability can be expressed as a percentage too.

- You should know how to convert fractions to percentages. Take a look again at lesson 6 if you've forgotten this.

- Remember to simplify your probability fraction if at all possible, as you saw in the example.

LESSON 7 PART 1

My Time My Score

Now look at the questions below. Work out the answers on some scrap paper and then mark them on the answer grids. Mark your time in the box provided once you've finished. Remember to get an adult to mark your answers. Then write your score in the box at the top of this page.

You have 10 minutes to complete these, so work quickly.

A A bookshelf contains 4 dictionaries, 2 books of maps, 8 story books, 6 poetry books and 5 picture books. If you pick out a book at random, what is the probability that you will pick a:

1 Picture book?

2 Book of maps?

3 Dictionary?

4 Poetry book?

5 Story book?

B A music player contains 4 jazz songs, 3 operatic songs, 9 pop songs, 6 rock songs and 8 rap songs. It selects songs at random. What is the probability it will pick a:

6 Rock song?

7 Rap song?

8 Jazz song?

9 Operatic song?

10 Pop song?

LESSON 7 PART 1: ANSWER SHEET

Mark your answer by putting a horizontal line in 1 of the boxes, as in the example below.

Example: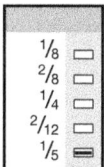

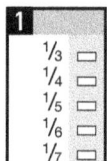  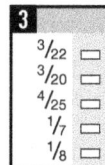

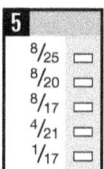  

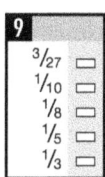 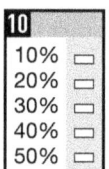

How Did You Do? Let's Find Out!

Remember, there is no self-marking in this book. Please get an adult to mark your answers.

If you scored 8 or more out of 10

This is a good score, well done. If you scored 8 or 9 try to improve on the next set of questions by checking where you went wrong and look below at the tips for speeding up before you move on.

If you scored fewer than 8 out of 10

To improve this score you should check the questions you got wrong and make sure you understand how to apply the method. You should also look below at the tips for speeding up before you move on.

TIPS FOR SPEEDING UP

- Make sure you're able to turn probability questions into fractions and simplify them quickly in your head (look back at lesson 4 to help with this).

- Make sure you can turn a fraction into a percentage quickly in your head (look back to lesson 6 to help with this).

LESSON 7 PART 2

My Time

My Score

Now let's try some more. Work the questions out on some scrap paper and then mark your answers on the answer sheet. Write the time you took and your score in the boxes above once you've finished. Remember to get an adult to mark these for you.

You have 10 minutes to complete these, so work quickly.

A A jar contains coins. It contains 12 × 10p, 8 × 20p, 7 × 2p, 14 × 1p and 9 × 50p coins. Picking a coin at random, what would be the probability of picking a:

1 50p?

2 10p?

3 2p?

4 20p?

5 1p?

B At the summer fair a game is played by spinning an arrow. What is the probability of spinning:

6 an odd number?

7 a number smaller than 6?

8 a 9?

9 a number larger than 4?

10 an even number?

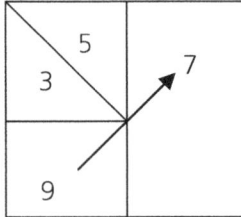

LESSON 7 PART 2: ANSWER SHEET

Mark your answer by putting a horizontal line in 1 of the boxes, as in the example below.

Example:

1/8	☐
2/8	☐
1/4	☐
2/12	☐
1/5	▬

1
9/41	☐
3/41	☐
6/41	☐
3/50	☐
9/50	☐

2
12/38	☐
12/62	☐
38/50	☐
6/25	☐
18/25	☐

3
7%	☐
14%	☐
21%	☐
28%	☐
35%	☐

4
8/28	☐
8/42	☐
4/46	☐
4/50	☐
4/25	☐

5
14/46	☐
14/64	☐
7/50	☐
7/25	☐
7/43	☐

6
50%	☐
70%	☐
80%	☐
90%	☐
100%	☐

7
2/6	☐
2/5	☐
2/4	☐
1/4	☐
1/8	☐

8
1/2	☐
1/3	☐
1/4	☐
1/5	☐
1/6	☐

9
25%	☐
40%	☐
50%	☐
75%	☐
87.5%	☐

10
certain	☐
possible	☐
likely	☐
unlikely	☐
impossible	☐

LESSON 8 Calculating Ratios

A ratio is a way of comparing the amount of one thing with another.

For example, I have two spoons of sugar for each cup of coffee I have. The ratio of spoons of sugar to cups of coffee is 2:1.

In this exercise, you'll need to use a ratio to help you calculate your answers. There are several types of ratio question. Let's remind ourselves of them with some examples.

Example 1

In a kitchen there are 14 plates and 8 cups.

The ratio of plates to cups is 14:8

Very occasionally, a question might expect you to simplify the answer above – just as you do with fractions (as seen in lesson 4). In this case, imagine the ratio is a fraction and find the largest number that will divide into both parts. In the case above it's 2 so you divide both parts by 2. Your final ratio then would be 7:4 and this is the one you would mark on your answer grid.

Example 2

The ratio on a farm of pigs to chickens is 2:3. If there are 16 pigs, how many chickens are there?

For the question above, 2 has been multiplied by 8 to get 16 pigs so you must also multiply the part of the ratio which represents chickens by 8. 3 × 8 is 24, so there are 24 chickens.

Example 3

A room contains 56 items of furniture in total and there are 6 chairs for every table. How many chairs are there?

For the question above you know that the ratio of chairs to tables is 6:1 so you would add these parts of the ratio. That's easy: 6 + 1 = 7. Now you divide the total items of furniture by this number, 56 ÷ 7 = 8. Finally you multiply each part of the original ratio by the answer you have just found:

Tables = 1 × 8 = 8

Chairs = 6 × 8 = 48

So there are 48 chairs. And as a final check, if you add 48 and 8 you get 56 which is the total number of items of furniture.

LESSON 8 PART 1

My Time My Score

Now look at the questions below. Work out the answers on some scrap paper and then mark them on the opposite page. Write the time you took in the box above once you've finished. Remember to get an adult to mark your answers. Then write your score in the box at the top of this page.

You have 10 minutes to complete these, so work quickly.

1 To bake a cake 6 eggs are needed. How many cakes can be baked if I have 36 eggs?

2 For every 3 blue flowers in a garden there are 7 yellow flowers. If the garden contains 21 blue flowers, how many yellow flowers are there?

3 Harry notices that for every sunny day there are 3 rainy days. How many rainy days are there in February in a non-leap year?

4 A garage sells 5 silver cars every time it sells a green car. If it sells 12 green cars, how many silver cars does it sell?

5 What is the ratio of vowels to consonants in the word RAINBOW?

6 A shop sells computer games. If it has 48 action games and 24 educational games, what is the ratio of action to educational games in its simplest form?

7 A book contains a picture page for every 20 pages of text. If it contains 9 pictures, how many pages does it contain in total?

8 A postman delivers 210 letters each morning. If the ratio of letters is 2 second class to 5 first class, how many first class letters does he deliver?

9 An office worker calculates that she receives 2 emails for every 7 she sends. In 1 day she sent 84 emails; how many did she receive?

10 A surveyor records that new houses are built with 7 windows to every 2 doors. If 22 new doors are ordered, how many windows will need to be ordered?

LESSON 8 PART 1: ANSWER SHEET

Mark your answer by putting a horizontal line in 1 of the boxes, as in the examples below.

Example 1:

```
7:4   ▬
8:14  ☐
6:8   ☐
8:6   ☐
14:22 ☐
```

Example 2:

```
21 ☐
11 ☐
18 ☐
19 ☐
24 ▬
```

Example 3:

```
8  ☐
56 ▬
7  ☐
15 ☐
41 ☐
```

1
```
30 ☐
42 ☐
6  ☐
12 ☐
18 ☐
```

2
```
28 ☐
31 ☐
21 ☐
49 ☐
42 ☐
```

3
```
10 ☐
13 ☐
14 ☐
21 ☐
28 ☐
```

4
```
60 ☐
84 ☐
17 ☐
12 ☐
7  ☐
```

5
```
3:7  ☐
4:7  ☐
3:4  ☐
3:10 ☐
4:10 ☐
```

6
```
2:3 ☐
4:1 ☐
5:1 ☐
2:1 ☐
3:1 ☐
```

7
```
180 ☐
181 ☐
189 ☐
29  ☐
129 ☐
```

8
```
203 ☐
21  ☐
40  ☐
70  ☐
150 ☐
```

9
```
4  ☐
14 ☐
24 ☐
34 ☐
44 ☐
```

10
```
14  ☐
37  ☐
46  ☐
77  ☐
115 ☐
```

How Did You Do? Let's Find Out!

Remember, there is no self-marking in this book. Please get an adult to mark your answers.

If you scored 8 or more out of 10

These types of ratio question should be fairly straightforward but you should still be careful. This is a good score but if you got 8 or 9 try to improve on the next set of questions by checking where you went wrong. Look below at the tips for speeding up before you move on.

If you scored fewer than 8 out of 10

You need to improve this result so check the questions you got wrong and make sure you understand the difference between the 3 types of question. Also read the tips for speeding up before you move on.

TIPS FOR SPEEDING UP

- There are lots of different types of question in this area. The best tip is to know your multiplication facts thoroughly.

- Watch out for the third type of question in the examples on page 61 which requires several steps to calculate the correct answer.

LESSON 8 PART 2

My Time

My Score

Now let's try some more. Work out the questions on some scrap paper and then mark your answers on the opposite page. Write the time you took and your score in the boxes above once you've finished. Again, remember that an adult needs to mark these for you.

You have 10 minutes to complete these, so work quickly.

1. A recipe for fruit salad requires 5 strawberries for every 4 grapes. If a fruit salad contains 40 grapes, how many strawberries does it require?

2. A class at school has a ratio of 7 girls to 4 boys. If there are 33 children in the class, how many are girls?

3. A football team coach calculates that for every goal the team concedes, it scores 3. If the team scores 123 goals in a season, how many does it concede?

4. Beth, Mia and Pauline raise money for a local charity. For every pound Beth raised, Mia raised 3 and Pauline raised 7. If they raised £132 between them, how much money did Mia raise?

5. A swimming pool needs 1 litre of cleaning fluid for every 80 litres of water. If it has 640 litres of water how much cleaning fluid is needed?

6. In a bakery there are 180 brown loaves and 90 white loaves. What is the ratio of brown to white loaves in its simplest form?

7. A radio station plays a song every 5 minutes. How many are played in an hour?

8. A farmer has 13 sheep for every 4 goats. If he has 102 animals in total, how many are goats?

9. In a gift shop there are 72 pencils and 54 key rings. What is the ratio of pencils to key rings in its simplest form?

10. A 'sloppy' ice cream is made with a ratio of 3:2 spoons of cream to ice. How many spoons of ice are needed for 15 'sloppy' ice-creams?

LESSON 8 PART 2: ANSWER SHEET

Mark your answer by putting a horizontal line in 1 of the boxes, as in the examples below.

Example 1:

7:4	▬
8:14	☐
6:8	☐
8:6	☐
14:22	☐

Example 2:

21	☐
11	☐
18	☐
19	☐
24	▬

Example 3:

8	☐
56	▬
7	☐
15	☐
41	☐

1
10	☐
20	☐
50	☐
160	☐
200	☐

2
5	☐
11	☐
21	☐
22	☐
28	☐

3
369	☐
41	☐
44	☐
120	☐
126	☐

4
£11	☐
£22	☐
£36	☐
£48	☐
£59	☐

5
56 litres	☐
72 litres	☐
8 litres	☐
10 litres	☐
16 litres	☐

6
90:1	☐
9:1	☐
2:1	☐
20:1	☐
3:1	☐

7
10	☐
11	☐
12	☐
13	☐
14	☐

8
9	☐
17	☐
24	☐
33	☐
41	☐

9
4:1	☐
4:2	☐
4:3	☐
4:4	☐
4:5	☐

10
10	☐
12	☐
13	☐
30	☐
45	☐

LESSON 9 Calculating Proportion

Proportion is the comparative relationship between two objects.

Often this is used in questions about costs. For example 1 pencil might cost 12p, so 2 would cost 24p. The cost is directly linked to the number of pencils and the proportion does not change no matter the amount of pencils.

In this exercise, you're given several pieces of information and you're required to work out a final piece. They can be a bit tricky and a sound knowledge of multiplication facts will help you identify patterns of numbers quickly. Let's look at some examples.

Example 1

If 8 football shirts cost £96, how much will 5 cost?

First find 1 shirt's cost by dividing £96 by 8.

96 ÷ 8 = 12.

Next multiply 12 by 5 to find the cost of 5 shirts. So 12 × 5 = 60. The cost of 5 shirts is £60.

Example 2

If a train travels 90km in 45 minutes, what speed is it travelling at in km/h?

This looks quite tricky but the actual numbers are not so bad; what makes it a bit more difficult is that you have several steps to complete. You solve it like this.

First begin with the time part. You need to know how many minutes are in 1 hour since you'll have to write the speed in this way. There are 60 minutes in 1 hour. You know how far the train travels in 45 minutes so you need to compare these 2 times. If you set these out as a fraction it looks like this $^{45}/_{60}$. And if you simplify this fraction (as you did in lesson 4) you are left with $^{3}/_{4}$.

You now know that $^{3}/_{4}$ is worth 90km so you can use your knowledge of finding a whole number from a fraction (lesson 3) to help you with the next step.

Divide the 90km by 3 which tells you what one-quarter is worth and then multiply it by 4 to get the whole number.

So the final sum would be 90 ÷ 3 = 30 and then 30 × 4 = 120.

The train is travelling at 120km/h.

LESSON 9 PART 1

My Time   **My Score**

Now look at the questions below. Work out the answers on some scrap paper and then mark them on the opposite page. Mark your time in the box provided once you've finished. Remember to get an adult to mark your answers. Then write your score in the box at the top of this page.

You have 10 minutes to complete these, so work quickly.

1. If 9 pencils cost 108p in total, how much money would 7 pencils cost?

2. A kilo of sugar costs £1.16; how much would 2.5kg cost?

3. If 5 football shirts cost £195 in total, how much would 3 cost?

4. In a restaurant 235 people were served over 5 hours. How many were served in 2 hours?

5. A telephone company charges its calls at £1.80 per hour. How much would a 20-minute call cost?

6. How much would 360ml of drink cost at 65p per 40ml?

7. If a cyclist travelled 90km in 3 hours, how far did she travel in 1½ hours?

8. In a warehouse 7 boxes weigh 112kg. How much would 4 boxes weigh?

9. If it takes a confectioner 90 minutes to ice 3 cakes, how long would it take to ice 2 cakes?

10. If a diamond weighing 21g costs £3,150, how much would a diamond weighing 14g cost?

LESSON 9 PART 1: ANSWER SHEET

Mark your answer by putting a horizontal line in 1 of the boxes, as in the examples below.

Example 1:

| £91 ☐ |
| £12 ☐ |
| £17 ☐ |
| £60 ▬ |
| £84 ☐ |

Example 2:

| 30km/h ☐ |
| 90km/h ☐ |
| 120km/h ▬ |
| 135km/h ☐ |
| 55km/h ☐ |

1
- 12p ☐
- 16p ☐
- 84p ☐
- 96p ☐
- 28p ☐

2
- £2.32 ☐
- £3.48 ☐
- £2.90 ☐
- £3.21 ☐
- £1.74 ☐

3
- £39 ☐
- £65 ☐
- £104 ☐
- £117 ☐
- £325 ☐

4
- 225 ☐
- 47 ☐
- 75 ☐
- 150 ☐
- 94 ☐

5
- £1.20 ☐
- £1.00 ☐
- 80p ☐
- 60p ☐
- 50p ☐

6
- £1.05 ☐
- £3.20 ☐
- £2.95 ☐
- £4.65 ☐
- £5.85 ☐

7
- 30km ☐
- 45km ☐
- 60km ☐
- 75km ☐
- 90km ☐

8
- 16kg ☐
- 28kg ☐
- 44kg ☐
- 64kg ☐
- 80kg ☐

9
- ¼ hour ☐
- ⅓ hour ☐
- ½ hour ☐
- ⅔ hour ☐
- 1 hour ☐

10
- £150 ☐
- £1,500 ☐
- £210 ☐
- £2,100 ☐
- £90 ☐

How Did You Do? Let's Find Out!

Remember, there is no self-marking in this book. Please get an adult to mark your answers.

If you scored 8 or more out of 10

This is a good score, well done. These types of proportion questions can be a little tricky, so read the question carefully, don't rush and you should be fine. If you got 8 or 9 try to improve on the next set of questions by checking where you went wrong and look below at the further hint and tips for speeding up before you move on.

If you scored fewer than 8 out of 10

These are tricky questions, but let's try to improve your score. Check the questions you got wrong and make sure you understand the difference between the types of question. Then read the further hint and tips for speeding up before you move on.

Further hint

Watch out for questions that mix units of measurement. A question may ask you to find the price of 50cm when you know the price of 1.5m. In this case you must make the link between centimetres and metres. Since there are 100cm in 1m you know that 1.5m is the same as 150cm. The question then becomes much easier. This can be done with all types of metric measurement.

TIPS FOR SPEEDING UP

- By using your knowledge of multiplication facts (times tables) you can check the relationships between numbers very quickly.

- Look at the possible answers on the answer sheet and try to eliminate any which are not reasonable – that is, they are far too big or too small. This will help you speed up.

LESSON 9 PART 2

My Time My Score

Now let's try some more. Work out the questions on some scrap paper and then mark your answers on the answer sheet. Write the time you took and your score in the boxes above once you've finished. Again, remember that an adult needs to mark your test for you.

You have 10 minutes to complete these, so work quickly.

1 If a crane moves 240 bricks in an hour, how many does it move in 80 minutes?

2 Apples cost £3.60 a dozen. How much do 7 cost?

3 Nick discovers he can answer 12 maths problems every 24 minutes. How long will it take him to answer 18 problems?

4 If 30 cartons weigh 4.5kg, how much do 20 cartons weigh?

5 Ilia calculates she reads 4 books every 3 weeks. How many books will she have read after 12 weeks?

6 If 1.2m of cloth costs 78p, how much would 2m cost?

7 A pedestrian walks 7 miles in 50 minutes. How far would he walk in 2½ hours?

8 If 4 containers hold 44 books, how many would 7 containers hold?

9 Football stickers come in packs of 12. How many packs did Ron buy to get 84?

10 What is the cost of 1.4kg of pears at 60p per 500g?

LESSON 9 PART 2: ANSWER SHEET

Mark your answer by putting a horizontal line in 1 of the boxes, as in the examples below.

Example 1:

- £91 ☐
- £12 ☐
- £17 ☐
- £60 ▬
- £84 ☐

Example 2:

- 30km/h ☐
- 90km/h ☐
- 120km/h ▬
- 135km/h ☐
- 55km/h ☐

1
- 30 ☐
- 160 ☐
- 320 ☐
- 400 ☐
- 480 ☐

2
- £1.80 ☐
- £2.10 ☐
- £2.40 ☐
- £2.70 ☐
- £3.00 ☐

3
- 30 minutes ☐
- 36 minutes ☐
- 42 minutes ☐
- 48 minutes ☐
- 54 minutes ☐

4
- 10kg ☐
- 6kg ☐
- 5kg ☐
- 3kg ☐
- 2kg ☐

5
- 7 ☐
- 12 ☐
- 15 ☐
- 16 ☐
- 23 ☐

6
- 81p ☐
- £1.30 ☐
- £1.80 ☐
- £2.00 ☐
- £2.10 ☐

7
- 43 miles ☐
- 14 miles ☐
- 41 miles ☐
- 21 miles ☐
- 12 miles ☐

8
- 48 ☐
- 51 ☐
- 58 ☐
- 65 ☐
- 77 ☐

9
- 3 ☐
- 4 ☐
- 5 ☐
- 6 ☐
- 7 ☐

10
- £3.00 ☐
- £1.68 ☐
- £1.64 ☐
- £1.56 ☐
- £1.52 ☐

LESSON 10 Calculating Volume

The volume of a shape is the amount of space it takes up.

In this exercise, you'll need to calculate the volume of a regular cube or cuboid. To do this, you multiply the length by the width by the height (LxWxH). Let's look at an example.

Example 1

Calculate the volume of the shape below.

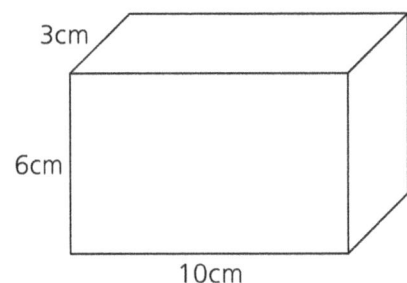

For the shape above, you need to multiply all 3 different measurements. You should do this in an organised way to make it as simple as possible. Multiplying by 10 is easy so leave that until last. First, find 6 × 3, which is 18. Now you can continue: 18 × 10 = <u>180cm</u>^{3}, which is the final answer.

Example 2

How many of the little cubes will fit into the large box?

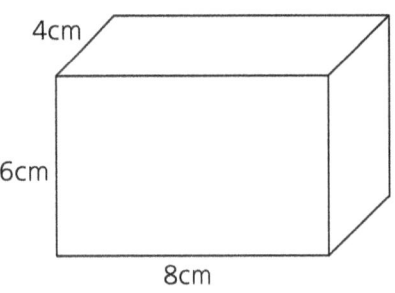 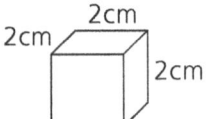

For these questions it's easier to compare each measurement of the 2 shapes. So first you can compare the lengths. The small cube is 2cm long whereas the large cuboid is 8cm long. So 4 cubes should fit along the length. Similarly, 3 cubes fit into the height and 2 the width. If you multiply these numbers you get 4 × 3 × 2 = <u>24</u> cubes, which is your final answer.

LESSON 10 PART 1

My Time

My Score

Now look at the questions below. Work out your answers on some scrap paper and then mark them on page 79. Mark your time in the box provided once you've finished. Remember to get an adult to mark your answers. Then write your score in the box at the top of this page.

You have 10 minutes to complete these, so work quickly.

1 A box measures 7cm long, 3cm wide and 5cm high. What is its volume?

2 A cube measures 6ft long. What is its volume?

3 If a room has a volume of 80m³ and has a length of 8m and a width of 5m, what is its height?

4 What is the volume of the shape below?

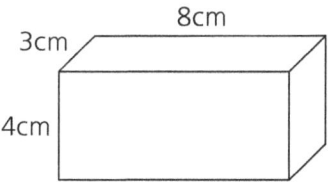

5 How many of box B will fit into box A?

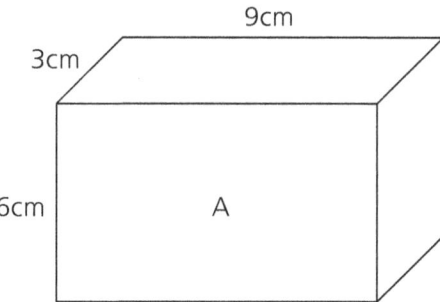
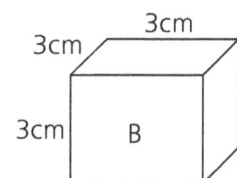

6 A container measures 9m by 7m by 6m. What is its volume?

7 If a bath measures 3m long by 2m wide and 1m deep, how many litres of water can it hold?

8 A factory has a volume of 1,750m³. If it is 35m long and 10m wide, what is its height?

9 What is side P worth if the volume of the box below is 480cm³?

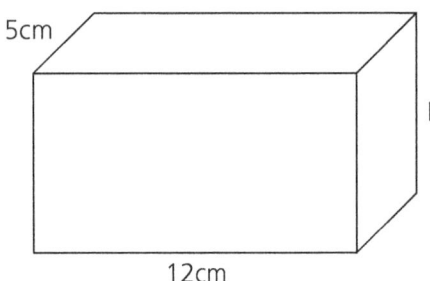

10 How many of box S will fit into box T?

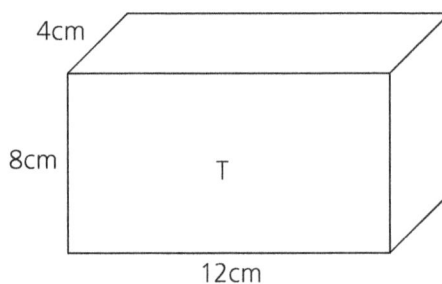 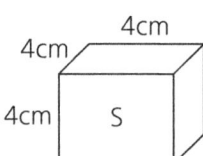

LESSON 10 PART 1: ANSWER SHEET

Mark your answer by putting a horizontal line in 1 of the boxes, as in the examples below.

Example 1:

- 120cm³ ☐
- 140cm³ ☐
- 160cm³ ☐
- 180cm³ ▬
- 200cm³ ☐

Example 2:

- 20 ☐
- 22 ☐
- 24 ▬
- 26 ☐
- 28 ☐

1
- 21cm³ ☐
- 35cm³ ☐
- 15cm³ ☐
- 105cm³ ☐
- 50cm³ ☐

2
- 36ft³ ☐
- 216ft³ ☐
- 24ft³ ☐
- 72ft³ ☐
- 126ft³ ☐

3
- 3,200m ☐
- 50m ☐
- 2m ☐
- 10m ☐
- 5m ☐

4
- 96cm³ ☐
- 84cm³ ☐
- 108cm³ ☐
- 32cm³ ☐
- 56cm³ ☐

5
- 27 ☐
- 9 ☐
- 6 ☐
- 12 ☐
- 18 ☐

6
- 70m³ ☐
- 63m³ ☐
- 54m³ ☐
- 350m³ ☐
- 378m³ ☐

7
- 2 litres ☐
- 3 litres ☐
- 4 litres ☐
- 5 litres ☐
- 6 litres ☐

8
- 350m ☐
- 30m ☐
- 20m ☐
- 10m ☐
- 5m ☐

9
- 60cm ☐
- 17cm ☐
- 420cm ☐
- 8cm ☐
- 10cm ☐

10
- 4 ☐
- 6 ☐
- 8 ☐
- 10 ☐
- 12 ☐

How Did You Do? Let's Find Out!

Remember, there is no self-marking in this book. Please get an adult to mark your answers.

If you scored 8 or more out of 10

These types of question should be straightforward provided you read the instructions carefully. There are several ways to ask about volume so just be wary. This is a good score but if you got 8 or 9 try to improve on the next set of questions by checking where you went wrong. Look below at the further hint and tip for speeding up before you move on.

If you scored fewer than 8 out of 10

You should be aiming to score at least 8 for these questions. Check the answers you got wrong and make sure you understand the extra step required to calculate volume. Then read the further hint and tip for speeding up before you move on to the next set of questions.

Further hint

You probably noticed that I reversed a few questions in the 10 you just finished. Questions 3, 8 and 9 all required you to divide the volume by the first measurement and then to divide that answer by the second measurement. Let's look at Question 3 again to show you what I mean.

> If a room has a volume of 80m³ and has a length of 8m and a width of 5m, what is its height?

So here you know what the volume is: 80m³. First divide 80 by 8 and the answer is 10. Next divide the 10 by 5 and the answer is 2. So the missing measurement is 2m. Just use the inverse operation – in other words, work backwards!

TIP FOR SPEEDING UP

When multiplying 3 numbers try to multiply the 2 most difficult ones first and keep the easy one for last. This will mean you can work faster with larger numbers – and will help you speed up.

LESSON 10 PART 2

My Time

My Score

Now let's try some more. Work out the questions on some scrap paper and then mark your answers on the answer sheet on page 83. Write the time you took and your score in the boxes above once you've finished. Remember to watch out for those questions which require inverse operations. When you're finished remember that an adult needs to mark these for you.

You have 10 minutes to complete these, so work quickly.

1 Carmel measures her toy box. It is 15cm wide, 3cm high and 30cm long. What is its volume?

2 A cube measures 12ft long. What is its volume?

3 If a room has a volume of 210m³ and its width is 5m and its height is 6m, what is its length?

4 What is the volume of the shape below?

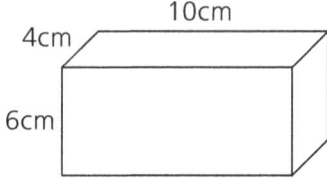

5 How many of box F will fit into box G?

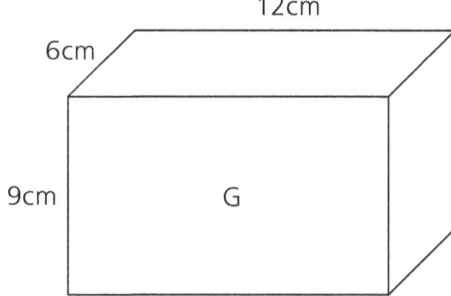 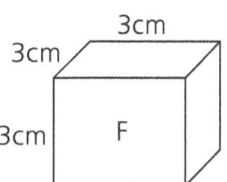

6 Ruby measures her cupboard. It is 3m wide, 4m high and 1m deep. Ruby estimates its volume is 10m³. By how many cubic metres is her estimate too small?

7 Look at the net of the shape below. If the shape was made, it would make an open box. What would its volume be?

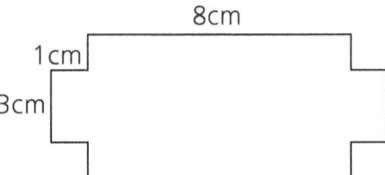

8 A factory has a volume of 3,996m³. If it is 37m long and 12m wide, what is its height?

9 What is side R worth if the volume of the box below is 630cm³

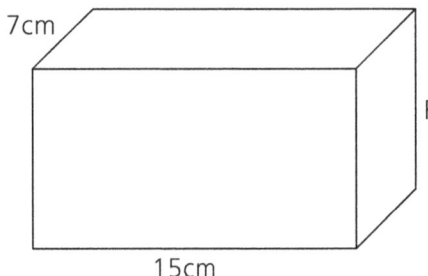

10 The volume of box C is 560cm³. How many of box D will fit into box C?

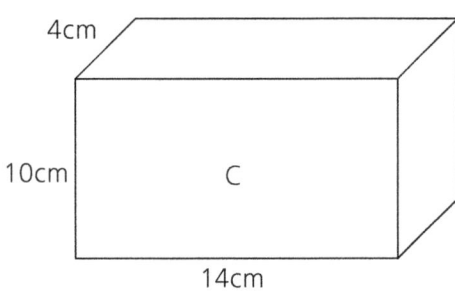 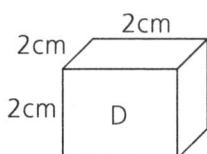

LESSON 10 PART 2: ANSWER SHEET

Mark your answer by putting a horizontal line in 1 of the boxes, as in the examples below.

Example 1:

120cm³	☐
140cm³	☐
160cm³	☐
180cm³	▬
200cm³	☐

Example 2:

20	☐
22	☐
24	▬
26	☐
28	☐

1
0.135cm³	☐
1.35cm³	☐
13.5cm³	☐
135cm³	☐
1,350cm³	☐

2
24ft³	☐
144ft³	☐
1,728ft³	☐
288ft³	☐
156ft³	☐

3
30m	☐
180m	☐
199m	☐
11m	☐
7m	☐

4
20cm³	☐
60cm³	☐
40cm³	☐
240cm³	☐
100cm³	☐

5
24	☐
12	☐
27	☐
9	☐
18	☐

6
1m³	☐
2m³	☐
3m³	☐
4m³	☐
35m³	☐

7
12cm³	☐
24cm³	☐
36cm³	☐
48cm³	☐
60cm³	☐

8
5m	☐
6m	☐
7m	☐
8m	☐
9m	☐

9
5cm	☐
6cm	☐
7cm	☐
8cm	☐
9cm	☐

10
50	☐
60	☐
70	☐
80	☐
90	☐

LESSON 11 Calculating the Area of Right-Angled Triangles and Irregular Shapes

In this exercise, you'll need to find the area of a right-angled triangle or an irregular shape. To calculate the area of a right-angled triangle, first find the measurement of the base of the triangle and halve it. Then multiply this number by the height of the triangle.

For other shapes, remember that normally you calculate the area of a rectangle or square by multiplying the length by the width (L × W). If a shape is not rectangular, (meaning it is an irregular shape) try to divide it into several rectangles or squares (as shown in example 2). Find the area of each and add the totals together.

Let's look at some examples.

Example 1

What is the area of the triangle below?

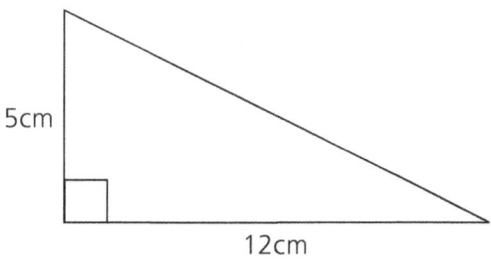

The base of this triangle is 12cm. So you halve it to make 6cm. Then you multiply this by the height which is 5cm.

So the area = 12 ÷ 2 = 6 × 5 = <u>30cm²</u>

Example 2

What is the area of the 'L' shape shown below?

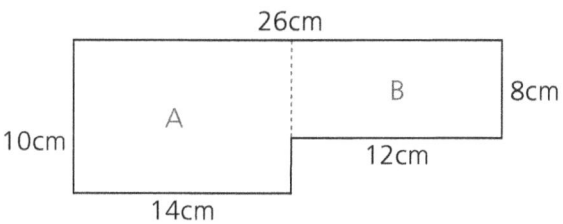

As this is an irregular shape the easiest thing to do is to divide it into 2 rectangles (which I have marked A and B). That way you can easily calculate the area of those shapes and add the totals together.

The area of shape A is 10cm × 14cm = 140cm².

The area of shape B is 8cm × 12cm = 96cm²

The total area is 140cm² + 96cm² = <u>236cm²</u>

LESSON 11 PART 1

My Time

My Score

Now look at the questions below. Work out the answers on some scrap paper and then mark them on the corresponding grids. Write the time you took in the box above once you've finished. Remember to get an adult to mark your answers. Then write your score in the box at the top of this page.

You have 10 minutes to complete these, so work quickly.

Find the area of the following shapes:

1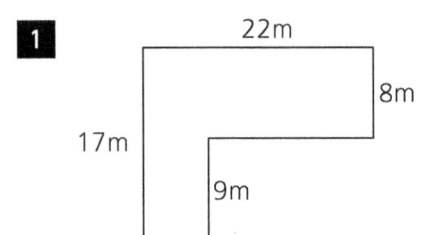

5

6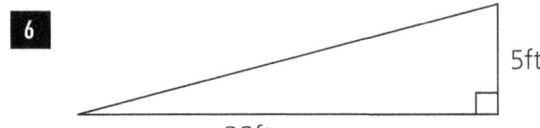

2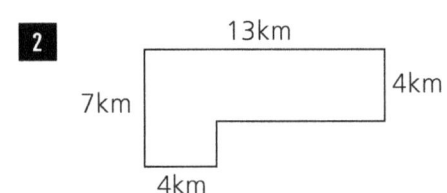

7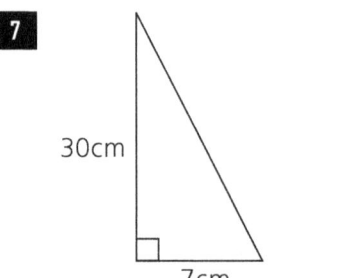

3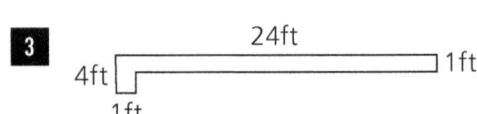

8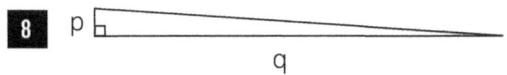

9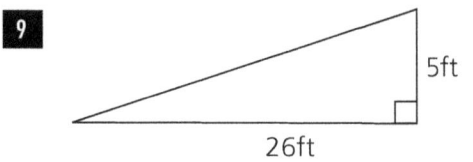

4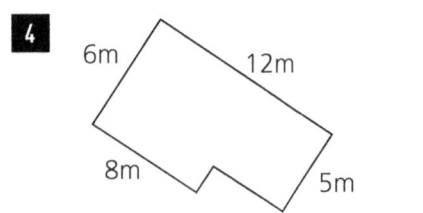

10 Find the perimeter of this shape.

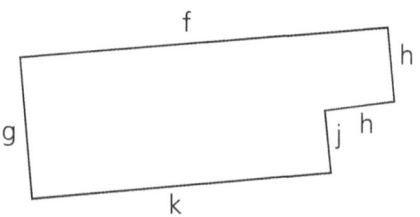

LESSON 11 PART 1: ANSWER SHEET

Mark your answer by putting a horizontal line in 1 of the boxes, as in the examples below.

Example 1:

- 28cm² ☐
- 30cm² ▬
- 32cm² ☐
- 34cm² ☐
- 36cm² ☐

Example 2:

- 96cm² ☐
- 140cm² ☐
- 236cm² ▬
- 206cm² ☐
- 44cm² ☐

1
- 44m² ☐
- 374m² ☐
- 329m² ☐
- 221m² ☐
- 176m² ☐

2
- 91km² ☐
- 80km² ☐
- 64km² ☐
- 52km² ☐
- 28km² ☐

3
- 30ft² ☐
- 29ft² ☐
- 28ft² ☐
- 27ft² ☐
- 26ft² ☐

4
- 60m² ☐
- 48m² ☐
- 12m² ☐
- 68m² ☐
- 72m² ☐

5
- 28m² ☐
- 132m² ☐
- 66m² ☐
- 94m² ☐
- 104m² ☐

6
- 23ft² ☐
- 33ft² ☐
- 140ft² ☐
- 70ft² ☐
- 52ft² ☐

7
- 210cm² ☐
- 37cm² ☐
- 44cm² ☐
- 52.5cm² ☐
- 105cm² ☐

8
- pq ☐
- p+q ☐
- p−q ☐
- pq×2 ☐
- pq÷2 ☐

9
- 21ft² ☐
- 31ft² ☐
- 105ft² ☐
- 65ft² ☐
- 130ft² ☐

10
- gk+hj ☐
- g+f+h+j+k ☐
- g+f+h+h+j+k ☐
- gf−hj ☐
- gk+2h ☐

How Did You Do? Let's Find Out!

Remember, there is no self-marking in this book. Please get an adult to mark your answers.

If you scored 8 or more out of 10

This is a good score but if you got 8 or 9 try to improve on the next set of questions by checking where you went wrong. Look below at the tips for speeding up before you move on.

If you scored fewer than 8 out of 10

These are quite straightforward questions so you should be scoring higher. Check the questions you got wrong and make sure you understand the methods required to calculate both types of question. Then look at the tips for speeding up before you move on to the next set of questions.

TIPS FOR SPEEDING UP

- Once again a thorough knowledge of multiplication facts is essential here. It will save you valuable time when you have several sets of multiplying to do.

- If you have to find the perimeter of an irregular shape, don't forget you must add all the sides and not just those with measurements shown. Work out the others and add them too.

LESSON 11 PART 2

My Time

My Score

Now let's try some more. Work out the questions on some scrap paper and then mark your answers on page 91. Write the time you took and your score in the boxes above once you've finished. Again, remember that an adult needs to mark these for you.

You have 10 minutes to complete these, so work quickly.

1 Find the perimeter of this shape.

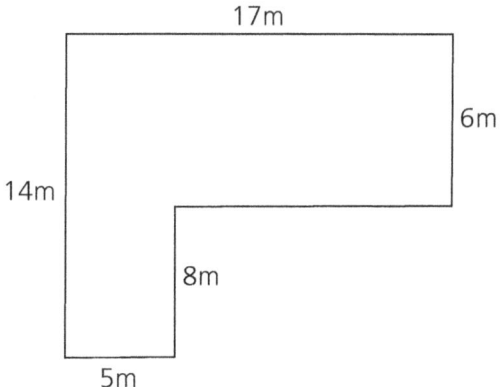

2 Find the area of this shape.

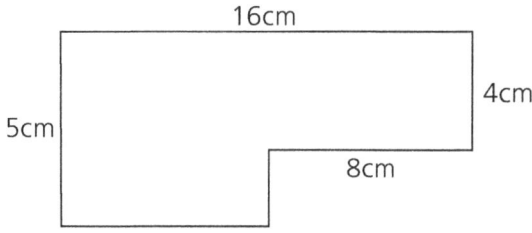

3 Find the perimeter of this shape.

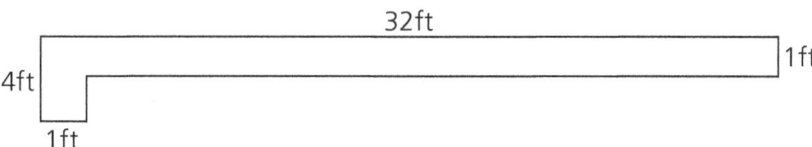

4 Find the area of this shape.

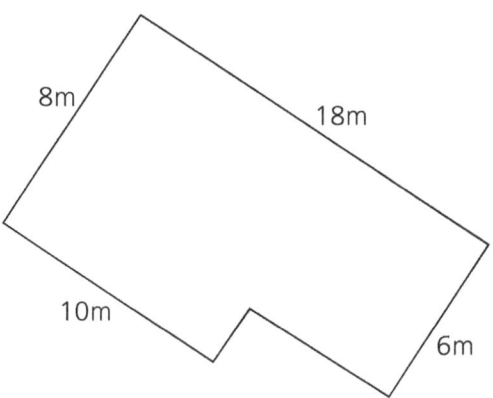

5 Find the perimeter of this shape.

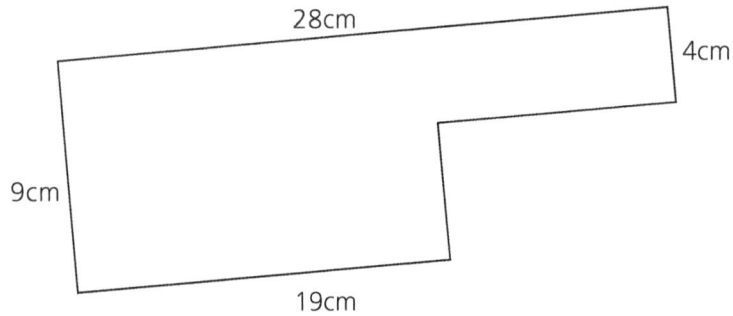

6 Find the area of this shape.

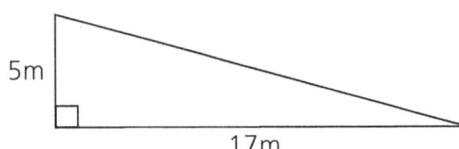

7 Find the area of this shape.

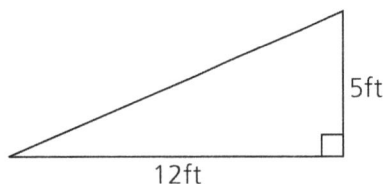

8 Find the area of this shape.

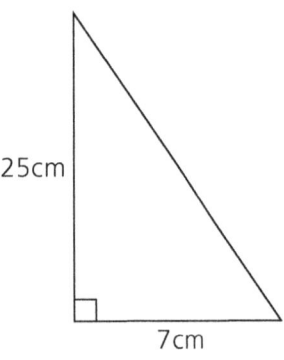

9 Find the area of this shape.

10 Find the area of this shape.

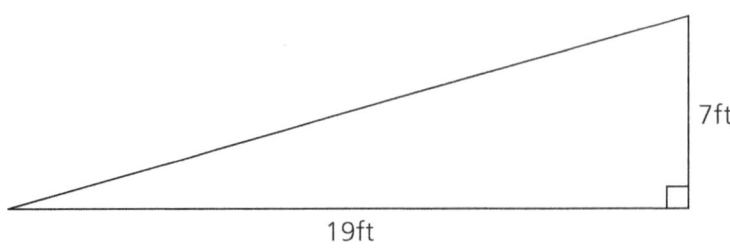

LESSON 11 PART 2: ANSWER SHEET

Mark your answer by putting a horizontal line in 1 of the boxes, as in the examples below.

Example 1:

- 28cm² ☐
- 30cm² ▬
- 32cm² ☐
- 34cm² ☐
- 36cm² ☐

Example 2:

- 96cm² ☐
- 140cm² ☐
- 236cm² ▬
- 206cm² ☐
- 44cm² ☐

1
- 60m ☐
- 61m ☐
- 62m ☐
- 63m ☐
- 64m ☐

2
- 33cm² ☐
- 53cm² ☐
- 72cm² ☐
- 90cm² ☐
- 102cm² ☐

3
- 65ft ☐
- 67ft ☐
- 69ft ☐
- 72ft ☐
- 73ft ☐

4
- 80m² ☐
- 104m² ☐
- 108m² ☐
- 118m² ☐
- 128m² ☐

5
- 60cm ☐
- 64cm ☐
- 68cm ☐
- 72cm ☐
- 74cm ☐

6
- 42.5m² ☐
- 22m² ☐
- 85m² ☐
- 45m² ☐
- 42m² ☐

7
- 15ft² ☐
- 20ft² ☐
- 25ft² ☐
- 30ft² ☐
- 35ft² ☐

8
- 175cm² ☐
- 125cm² ☐
- 100cm² ☐
- 90cm² ☐
- 87.5cm² ☐

9
- 100m² ☐
- 110m² ☐
- 120m² ☐
- 130m² ☐
- 140m² ☐

10
- 66.5ft² ☐
- 67.5ft² ☐
- 68.5ft² ☐
- 69.5ft² ☐
- 70.5ft² ☐

LESSON 12 Reading Information from Graphs

In this exercise, you'll need to find some information from a graph and then use it to calculate your answer. These questions should be fairly straightforward if you look at the graph carefully. Many of the problems happen when students go too fast and don't read the question properly. Let's look at an example.

Example

How many more oak trees are there than ash trees?

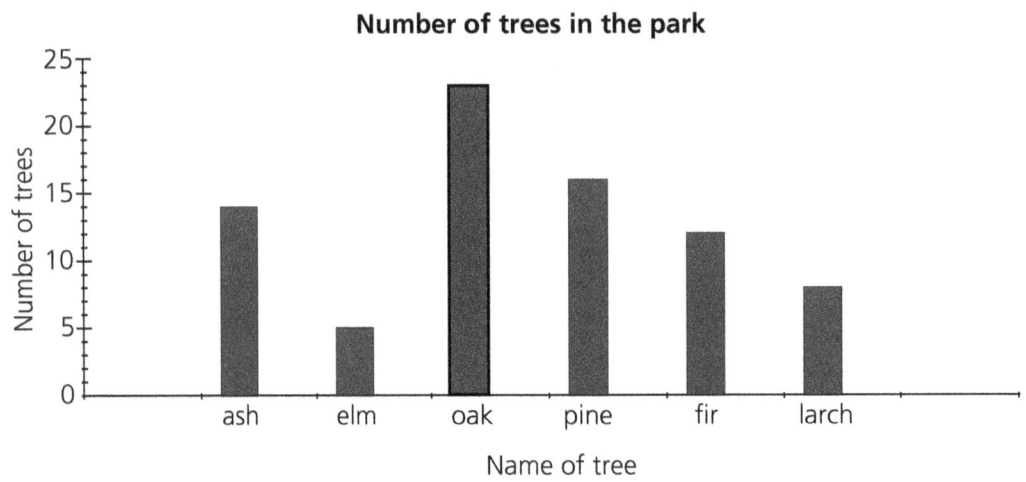

For the question above, you need to find out how many oak and how many ash trees there are using the graph. The oak tree column is between 20 and 25 so use your ruler to get an accurate reading. Doing this, you find that there are 23 oak trees. Do the same to help you find the number of ash trees, which is 14. Now you must subtract 14 from 23.

23 – 14 = 9, so there are 9 more oak trees than ash trees.

LESSON 12 PART 1

My Time

My Score

Now look at the questions below. Use your ruler to help you find information from the graph correctly and then mark your answers on page 95. Write the time you took in the box above once you've finished. Remember to get an adult to mark your answers. Then write your score in the box at the top of this page.

You have 10 minutes to complete these, so work quickly.

A The graph below shows people's favourite pizza toppings. Answer questions 1–3 using this graph.

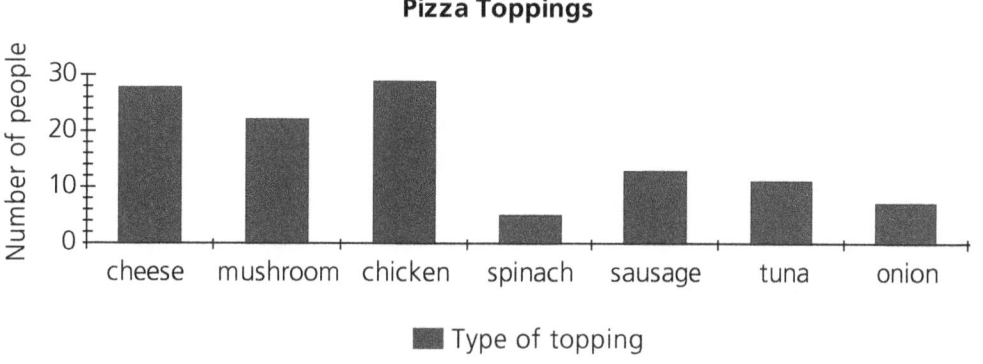

1 How many pizza toppings were liked by more than 20 people?

2 How many more people liked chicken than tuna?

3 How many people wanted sausage as a topping?

B The graph below shows the children at each age in a school. Use this graph to answer questions 4–6

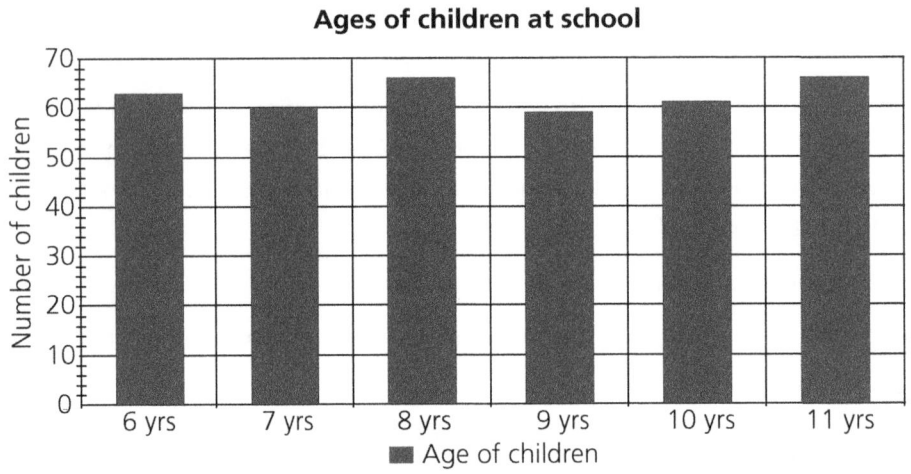

4 Which 2 ages had the same number of students?

5 Which age had the least number of students?

6 How many 6 and 7 year olds are there all together?

C The graph below shows how many children liked each animal the most at the zoo. Use this graph to answer questions 7–10.

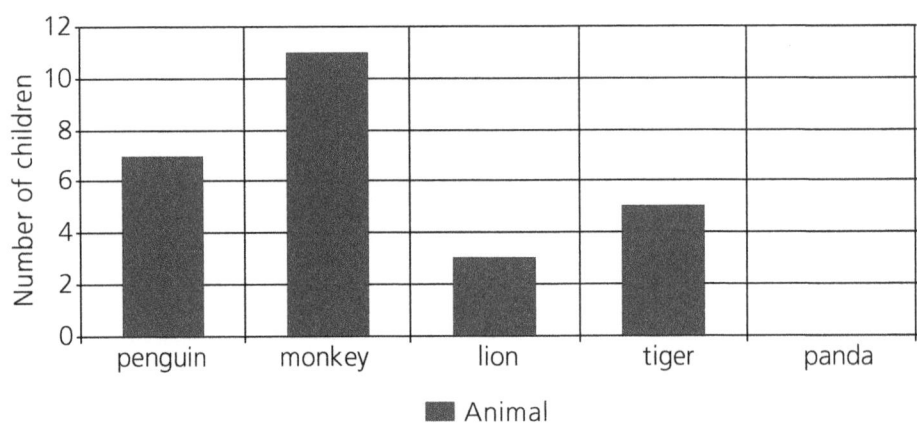

7 When drawing the graph, the teacher forgot to put the bar for those children who liked the panda most. If 32 children were surveyed in all, how many liked the panda the most?

8 What is the difference in votes between the most popular and least popular animal?

9 Which animal had an even number of children vote for it?

10 How many children liked one of the big cats the most?

LESSON 12 PART 1: ANSWER SHEET

Mark your answer by putting a horizontal line in 1 of the boxes, as in the example below.

Example:

```
8  □
9  ▭
10 □
11 □
12 □
```

1
```
30 □
6  □
5  □
4  □
3  □
```

2
```
30 □
12 □
19 □
7  □
25 □
```

3
```
10 □
20 □
30 □
13 □
25 □
```

4
```
6 and 7 years  □
7 and 8 years  □
7 and 11 years □
8 and 11 years □
9 and 10 years □
```

5
```
6 years  □
7 years  □
8 years  □
9 years  □
10 years □
```

6
```
123 □
100 □
150 □
223 □
120 □
```

7
```
2  □
4  □
6  □
8  □
10 □
```

8
```
5 □
6 □
7 □
8 □
9 □
```

9
```
panda   □
penguin □
monkey  □
lion    □
tiger   □
```

10
```
5 □
6 □
7 □
8 □
9 □
```

How Did You Do? Let's Find Out!

Remember, there is no self-marking in this book. Please get an adult to mark your answers.

If you scored 8 or more out of 10

This is a good result. These types of questions should be ones you score well on if you find the information you need from the graphs carefully. If you scored 8 or 9 try to improve on the next set of questions by checking where you went wrong. Look below at the further hints and tips for speeding up before you move on.

If you scored fewer than 8 out of 10

You should be scoring high on these questions. Try taking a look back at the questions you got wrong. Also check that you didn't make a mistake when putting your answers on the sheet. Read the further hints and the tips for speeding up before moving on to the next set of questions.

Further hints

⇨ Did you notice on question 7 that once again you had to reverse the operations? Having been told that there were 32 children in the survey, you needed to add all the other votes together and take the answer away from 32. So 7 + 11 + 3 + 5 = 26 and 32 − 26 = 6.

⇨ Remember that graphs can take different forms and that data (information) can also be shown in tables. Practise using as many different types of graphs as you can to get used to finding information from all types.

TIPS FOR SPEEDING UP

- Make sure you read the question carefully and answer the question being asked, not what you think is being asked.
- Make sure you read the scale on each graph carefully.
- Use your ruler to help you read the graph correctly and then mark your answers on the grid.

LESSON 12 PART 2

My Time

My Score

Now let's try some more. Mark your answers on the corresponding answer grids, which can be found on page 101. Write the time you took and your score in the boxes above once you've finished. Again, remember that an adult needs to mark these for you.

You have 10 minutes to complete these, so work quickly.

A The table below shows how many students chose each after-school activity. Use it to answer question 1.

Football	Yoga	Swimming	Craft	Drama	Dancing	Guitar
33	?	27	9	14	17	5

1 If there were 120 students in total, how many chose yoga?

B The pie chart below shows the motor car colours people prefer to buy. Use it to answer question 2.

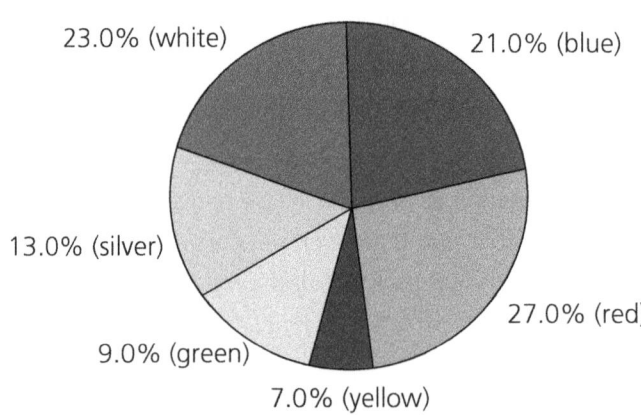

23.0% (white)
21.0% (blue)
13.0% (silver)
9.0% (green)
7.0% (yellow)
27.0% (red)

2 The colour of each car is given in brackets by each percentage. Which was the least popular colour?

C Look at the table below and use it to answer questions 3–5.

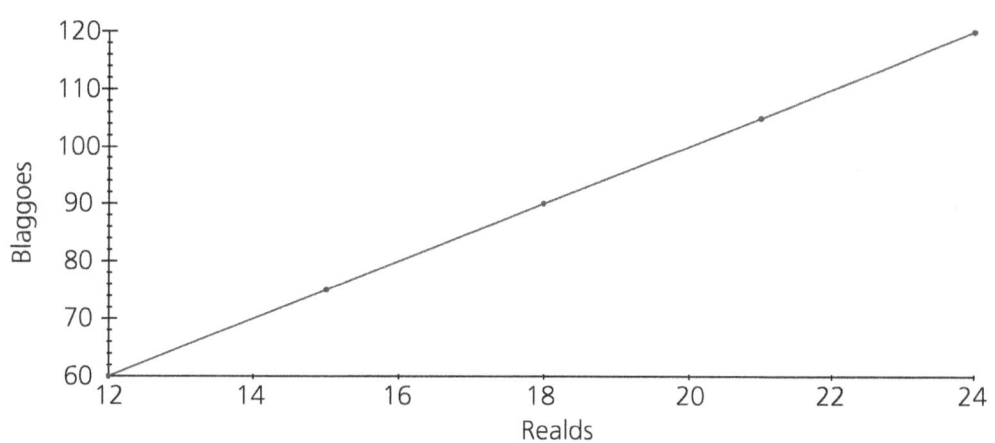

3 How many people took part in the survey altogether?

4 What percentage of the people surveyed preferred strawberry flavour?

5 How many more people preferred chocolate to pistachio?

D Look at the graph below showing the conversion rate of 2 fictional currencies. Use it to answer questions 6 and 7.

6 How many blaggoes would you get for 20 realds?

7 How many blaggoes would you get for 36 realds?

E Look at the graph below showing the musical instruments played by students at a school play. Use it to answer questions 8–10.

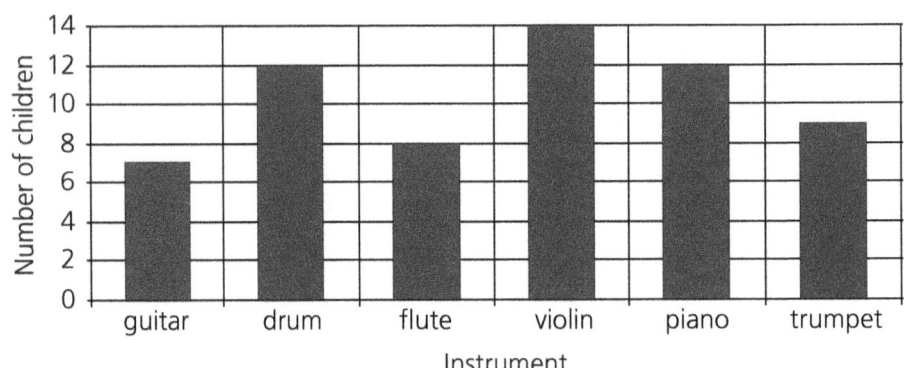

8 Which 2 instruments were played by the same number of students?

9 How many more students played piano than guitar?

10 How many students played instruments in total?

LESSON 12 PART 2: ANSWER SHEET

Mark your answer by putting a horizontal line in 1 of the boxes, as in the example below.

Example:

```
 8 ☐
 9 ▬
10 ☐
11 ☐
12 ☐
```

1
```
14 ☐
15 ☐
16 ☐
17 ☐
18 ☐
```

2
```
silver ☐
white  ☐
green  ☐
yellow ☐
red    ☐
```

3
```
10 ☐
20 ☐
30 ☐
40 ☐
50 ☐
```

4
```
10% ☐
20% ☐
30% ☐
40% ☐
50% ☐
```

5
```
1 ☐
2 ☐
3 ☐
4 ☐
8 ☐
```

6
```
 18 ☐
 22 ☐
 90 ☐
100 ☐
110 ☐
```

7
```
 18 ☐
 90 ☐
180 ☐
 36 ☐
 12 ☐
```

8
```
guitar, drum ☐
piano, drum  ☐
piano, flute ☐
violin, flute ☐
flute, drum  ☐
```

9
```
12 ☐
 7 ☐
 6 ☐
 5 ☐
 4 ☐
```

10
```
60 ☐
61 ☐
62 ☐
63 ☐
64 ☐
```

LESSON 13 Multiplying Larger Numbers

> **IMPORTANT!**
>
> When multiplying larger numbers, you'll be depending totally on your knowledge of multiplication facts (times tables). So it's vital that your knowledge is absolutely water-tight. I know a lot of students think 'counting up' in multiples is good enough. I agree it's a useful skill but remember that it simply isn't good enough on its own. If I ask you what 9 × 7 is for example, I would expect you to be able to answer within 2 seconds. If you can't do this, you'll need to take care of this now.

In this exercise you'll be multiplying larger numbers. There are several methods you can use to do this. The one I will show you here is very traditional but can be done very quickly – which is the reason I've chosen it. Remember, you will only get 1 minute for each question so you want a fast, efficient method. If you find it difficult, either practise it until you perfect it or use another method that you are more comfortable with, but make sure you work accurately and at speed.

Let's look at an example.

Example

What is 28 × 345?

This method multiplies one part at a time then adds the totals to get the final answer.

```
    3 4 5
  ×   2 8
= 2 7₃6₄0
+ 6 9₁0 0
= 9₁6 6 0
```

First multiply 8 by 5, then by 4 and then by 3; carry amounts over to the next place value column where necessary.

Then on the line underneath put a 0 in the units column and multiply 2 by 5, 4, and 3 placing your answers to the left of the units column.

Add the totals to get the final answer.

So what are you actually doing with this method? Let's take a closer look.

You start with 8 × 5   = 40
then   8 × 40 = 320
then   8 × 300 = 2,400

But instead of writing all these out, you add them as you go along.

Once you know that 8 × 5 = 40 you can write 0 in the units and carry 4 into the tens column.

This means that you don't need to multiply 8 by 40 but instead can multiply 8 by 4. The answer to 8 × 4 is 32 and then you add the 4 you have already carried into the tens column, giving 36.

You then write 6 in the tens column and carry 3 across to the hundreds column. You complete this row by simply multiplying 8 by 3 which is 24. You add the 3 you carried to the hundreds column previously and find the answer is 27.

Since there are no other digits to multiply, you write the number in making sure the 7 is in the hundreds and the 2 is in the thousands.

So the first row is 2,760.

You continue with the next row in the same way except for one important point. This time you are multiplying by 20. To make this easier, you know that whenever you multiply by a number ending in 0, the answer will also end in 0. So in this case you simply put a 0 in the units column and multiply each of the top numbers by 2 in the usual way.

If you had a third row to do you would be multiplying by hundreds and so would put a 0 in the units column and the tens column before continuing.

So the second row is 6,900.

Then you add the 2 rows together and get the final answer which is 9,660.

If you're unsure at any stage of this working out, get an adult to work through it with you and show you how the method works.

LESSON 13 PART 1

My Time

My Score

Now look at the questions below. Work out the answers on some scrap paper and then mark them on the corresponding grids. Mark your time in the box provided when you've finished. Remember to get an adult to mark your answers. Then write your score in the box at the top of this page.

You have 10 minutes to complete these, so work quickly.

1. A garden has 39 rows of flowers and 67 flowers in each row. How many flowers are there all together?

2. A store has 76 shelves and 54 tins stacked on each shelf. How many tins are there in total?

3. If 23 children each have collected 89 stickers, how many stickers do they have all together?

4. 77 buses leave the depot one morning. If each bus carries 45 people, how many people can they carry in all?

5. If 12 books each contain 756 pages, how many pages are there in all the books?

6. 64 aeroplanes took off from an airport, each carrying 237 passengers. How many passengers took off in total?

7. If 42 cars contain a total of 1,470 litres of petrol, how many litres does each car hold?

8. A darts player scores 1,020 points with 17 darts. How many points does he score with each dart?

9. If 273 houses each spend £47 on food each week, how much money is spent in total?

10. A car travelled 6,318 miles in 27 days. How many miles did it travel each day?

LESSON 13 PART 1: ANSWER SHEET

Mark your answer by putting a horizontal line in 1 of the boxes, as in the example below.

Example:

9,660	▬
9,066	☐
9,606	☐
6,906	☐
6,609	☐

1
- 2,613 ☐
- 273 ☐
- 2,340 ☐
- 2,730 ☐
- 507 ☐

2
- 3,040 ☐
- 4,104 ☐
- 3,240 ☐
- 4,332 ☐
- 3,780 ☐

3
- 1,780 ☐
- 1,840 ☐
- 445 ☐
- 207 ☐
- 2,047 ☐

4
- 3,150 ☐
- 315 ☐
- 3,850 ☐
- 4,165 ☐
- 3,465 ☐

5
- 7,560 ☐
- 1,512 ☐
- 9,072 ☐
- 9,048 ☐
- 8,048 ☐

6
- 14,220 ☐
- 9,480 ☐
- 2,368 ☐
- 9,408 ☐
- 15,168 ☐

7
- 31 litres ☐
- 33 litres ☐
- 35 litres ☐
- 37 litres ☐
- 39 litres ☐

8
- 30 ☐
- 40 ☐
- 50 ☐
- 60 ☐
- 70 ☐

9
- £10,920 ☐
- £19,110 ☐
- £10,800 ☐
- £12,831 ☐
- £12,381 ☐

10
- 230 miles ☐
- 231 miles ☐
- 232 miles ☐
- 233 miles ☐
- 234 miles ☐

How Did You Do? Let's Find Out!

Remember, there is no self-marking in this book. Please get an adult to mark your answers.

If you scored 8 or more out of 10

This is a good score but if you got 8 or 9 try to improve on the next set of questions. Check where you went wrong and then look below at the further hint and tip for speeding up before you move on.

If you scored fewer than 8 out of 10

Check the questions you got wrong. Make sure that you didn't make a mistake when putting your answers on the sheet. Always check that your answer is reasonable. If you think it is but it isn't included on the answer grid you'll need to check your working. Read the further hint and tip for speeding up and then move on to the next set of questions.

Further hint

Did you notice that questions 7, 8 and 10 required you to use the inverse operation again, in other words you need to use the opposite method to the one used in the other questions. The inverse of multiplying is dividing so make sure you've practised this skill too – it's bound to be needed at some point!

For example, for question 7, 1,470 needs to be divided by 42 to get the correct answer. Don't multiply 1,470 by 42 as this would give you an answer that is neither on the grid, nor reasonable!

TIP FOR SPEEDING UP

Try to use the method I've shown you for these – it's quicker than others you may have come across, such as splitting numbers up into boxes.

LESSON 13 PART 2

My Time

My Score

Now let's try some more. Work out the questions on some scrap paper and then mark your answers on the answer sheet. Write the time you took and your score in the boxes above once you've finished. Again, remember that an adult needs to mark these for you.

You have 10 minutes to complete these, so work quickly.

1. A cinema sold 312 tickets per day for 14 days. How many tickets did it sell in total?

2. A ferry carried a total of 5,484 people spread equally over 12 trips. How many people did it carry on each trip?

3. If a school has 32 children in each of 16 classes, how many children does it have all together?

4. Barry counts that there are 342 words on each page of his book. If his book has 123 pages, how many words are there in total?

5. If a coach of 49 people carries a total of 1,617kg of luggage, how much does each person's luggage weigh?

6. 14 water tanks each hold 33 litres of water. How much water is that in total?

7. A factory produces 167 cars every day for 2 weeks including weekends. How many cars does it produce in this time altogether?

8. An office employs 37 people. If each one works 45 hours in a week, how many hours is that in total?

9. If 17 tins of paint covered a total of 1,088 fence panels, how many panels can 1 tin cover?

10. A company recycles 262 bottles in a day. How many is this in 50 days?

LESSON 13 PART 2: ANSWER SHEET

Mark your answer by putting a horizontal line in 1 of the boxes, as in the example below.

Example:

9,660 ▬
9,066 ▭
9,606 ▭
6,906 ▭
6,609 ▭

1
4,368 ▭
3,120 ▭
4,200 ▭
4,340 ▭
4,228 ▭

2
455 ▭
456 ▭
457 ▭
458 ▭
459 ▭

3
320 ▭
480 ▭
450 ▭
512 ▭
521 ▭

4
41,040 ▭
41,820 ▭
36,900 ▭
42,066 ▭
35,226 ▭

5
30kg ▭
31kg ▭
32kg ▭
33kg ▭
34kg ▭

6
330 litres ▭
363 litres ▭
396 litres ▭
429 litres ▭
462 litres ▭

7
2,240 ▭
1,670 ▭
2,324 ▭
2,338 ▭
2,004 ▭

8
1,565 ▭
1,665 ▭
1,656 ▭
1,556 ▭
1,566 ▭

9
60 ▭
61 ▭
62 ▭
63 ▭
64 ▭

10
13,000 ▭
13,100 ▭
13,200 ▭
13,300 ▭
13,400 ▭

LESSON 14 Finding Averages and Ranges

In this exercise, you'll need to calculate or use one of the 3 types of average or a range to work out your answer. Make sure that you understand the difference between each type and how to calculate them. Let's remind ourselves of what each type of average and the range means.

Mean

This type of average requires you to add up all the numbers that you have been given and then divide your answer by the amount of numbers. So, if the sum of 11 numbers is 55, the mean is 5 ($55 \div 11 = 5$).

Median

This type of average requires you to place all the numbers you have in order of size from the smallest to the biggest. Where a number occurs more than once, you must write it more than once. Then you simply count along and find the number that appears in the middle of the list. If there is no one number in the middle you must take the 2 numbers which are closest and find the mean of these (add them and divide them by 2).

Mode

This type of average is similar to the median in that you should first place all the numbers in order of size from smallest to biggest. Then you simply check which number occurs most often and that number is the mode.

Range

The range isn't an average. It simply tells you the difference between the largest and smallest number you have. So you simply subtract the smallest number from the largest.

HELPFUL HINTS

- If a question simply states: 'find the average', use the mean.

- If you've forgotten how to work out any of these, go back to lesson 14 in the first book in this series (*Practise & Pass Level One: Discover Maths*) where I've given examples for each type.

LESSON 14 PART 1

My Time | **My Score**

Now look at the questions below. Work out the answers on some scrap paper and then mark them on the corresponding grids. Mark your time in the box provided when you've finished. Remember to get an adult to mark your answers. Then write your score in the box at the top of this page.

You have 10 minutes to complete these, so work quickly.

1 Three roads measure 15km, 19km and 17km. What is their average length?

2 5 bottles hold 200ml, 320ml, 315ml, 470ml and 590ml. What is the median of these amounts?

3 Rick collects stamps and counted how many he collected each day for 1 week. He collected: 12, 7, 5, 9, 8, 6 and 7. Which number represents the mode?

4 Applicants for a job took a test out of 20 and scored 11, 14, 6, 15, 17 and 19. What is the range of their scores?

5 In a busy market, traders are selling cartons of mushrooms. What is the median number of mushrooms per carton of the following: 21, 32, 40, 40 and 34?

6 Arnold counts that the number of birds visiting his garden each day for a week is 17, 6, 18, 5, 18, 6 and 18. What is the mode?

7 What is the mean of the following number of pages in books: 227, 103, 258, 386 and 441?

8 Find the range of the following amounts of money: £2.09, £5.65, £6.86, £3.23 and £4.87.

9 A farmer sells 24, 36, 42, 61, 23, 39 and 45 eggs on each day of the week. What is the range?

10 A shop sells 15 red, 31 blue, 12 green, 45 white and 34 black hats. Which colour represents the median?

LESSON 14 PART 1: ANSWER SHEET

Mark your answer by putting a horizontal line in 1 of the boxes for each answer.

1
- 15km ☐
- 16km ☐
- 17km ☐
- 18km ☐
- 19km ☐

2
- 200ml ☐
- 320ml ☐
- 315ml ☐
- 470ml ☐
- 590ml ☐

3
- 5 ☐
- 6 ☐
- 7 ☐
- 8 ☐
- 9 ☐

4
- 6 ☐
- 8 ☐
- 13 ☐
- 14 ☐
- 15 ☐

5
- 21 ☐
- 32 ☐
- 40 ☐
- 34 ☐
- 33 ☐

6
- 5 ☐
- 6 ☐
- 7 ☐
- 17 ☐
- 18 ☐

7
- 227 ☐
- 238 ☐
- 258 ☐
- 283 ☐
- 328 ☐

8
- £1.77 ☐
- £2.77 ☐
- £3.77 ☐
- £4.77 ☐
- £5.77 ☐

9
- 32 ☐
- 34 ☐
- 36 ☐
- 38 ☐
- 40 ☐

10
- white ☐
- red ☐
- green ☐
- black ☐
- blue ☐

How Did You Do? Let's Find Out!

Remember, there is no self-marking in this book. Please get an adult to mark your answers.

If you scored 8 or more out of 10

This is a good result but if you scored 8 or 9 you should try to improve on the next set of questions. Check where you went wrong and look at the further hint below before you move on.

If you scored fewer than 8 out of 10

Try and improve this score for the next set of questions. Check the questions you got wrong and make sure that you didn't make a mistake when putting your answers on the sheet. Read the further hint below and then move on to the next set of questions.

Further hint

Do you understand how to calculate each type of average and also the range? Make sure you learn them all thoroughly before you proceed. Some people use the following rhyme to help:

Hey diddle diddle, the median's the middle,
Add then divide for the mean.
The mode is the one you can see the most,
And the range is the difference in between.

LESSON 14 PART 2

My Time **My Score**

Now let's try some more. Work out the questions on some scrap paper and then mark your answers on the corresponding grids. Write the time you took and your score in the boxes above once you've finished. Remember to get an adult to mark these for you.

You have 10 minutes to complete these, so work quickly.

1. A car drives the following number of kilometres each day for a week: 17, 35, 43, 57, 58, 44 and 67. What is the median distance it travels?

2. CDs in a shop cost £3.99, £4.24, £1.98 and £1.79. What is the mean price?

3. If the range of a car's speed is 69mph and the slowest it recorded was 17mph, what was the fastest speed it recorded?

4. Five television programmes lasted 35 minutes, 47 minutes, half an hour, 1 hour and 73 minutes. What was their median length?

5. Five buildings measure 149ft, 1,002ft, 865ft, 903ft and 856ft. What is their median height?

6. The total weight of 7 people is 560kg. What is their average weight?

7. The number of tickets sold for an amateur concert each night of the week is as follows: Monday 123, Tuesday 245, Wednesday 236, Thursday 245, Friday 162, Saturday 267 and Sunday 120. What is the mode?

8. The average amount of money children on a trip have to spend is £4.50. If Bob has £3.75 and Kyle has £6.20, how much does Emma have?

9. Amal measured the temperature in her room for 5 days at: 9°C, 13°C, 20°C, 13°C, and 25°C. What is the median of these?

10. Find the range of these numbers: 3.02, 5.76, 4.43, 5.23, 6.7 and 1.39.

LESSON 14 PART 2: ANSWER SHEET

Mark your answer by putting a horizontal line in 1 of the boxes for each answer.

1
- 35km ☐
- 43km ☐
- 44km ☐
- 57km ☐
- 58km ☐

2
- £1.50 ☐
- £2.00 ☐
- £2.50 ☐
- £3.00 ☐
- £3.50 ☐

3
- 82mph ☐
- 83mph ☐
- 84mph ☐
- 85mph ☐
- 86mph ☐

4
- 35 minutes ☐
- 47 minutes ☐
- 1/2 hour ☐
- 1 hour ☐
- 73 minutes ☐

5
- 149ft ☐
- 1,002ft ☐
- 865ft ☐
- 903ft ☐
- 856ft ☐

6
- 50kg ☐
- 60kg ☐
- 70kg ☐
- 80kg ☐
- 90kg ☐

7
- 123 ☐
- 245 ☐
- 236 ☐
- 162 ☐
- 267 ☐

8
- £3.50 ☐
- £3.55 ☐
- £3.60 ☐
- £3.65 ☐
- £3.70 ☐

9
- 9°C ☐
- 13°C ☐
- 20°C ☐
- 25°C ☐
- 12°C ☐

10
- 5.31 ☐
- 5.32 ☐
- 5.33 ☐
- 5.34 ☐
- 5.35 ☐

LESSON 15 Finding a Percentage of a Number

In this exercise, you'll need to use your knowledge of the factors of 100 to help you calculate percentages quickly. Remember that the % sign means 'in every hundred'. If you're not sure about factors or percentages look back at *Level One: Discover Maths*, lesson 15.

Remember, the factors of 100 are: 1, 2, 4, 5, 10, 20, 25, 50, 100 and they all pair up to make 100. So, 1 x 100, 2 x 50, 4 x 25, 5 x 20, and then 10 x 10.

Let's look at an example.

Example

Find 20% of the number 250.

How do you find 20% of something? Think of the pair of 20 in the factors of 100. Its pair is 5 (because 20 x 5 =100), so you divide the number by 5.

20% of 250 = 250 ÷ 5 = 50.

HELPFUL HINT

If you're asked to find 15% try finding 10% first, then halving the answer and adding the 2 parts together.

Example 2

Carl gets a 15% discount on a new television which usually costs £240.

How much money did he save?

To solve the problem above first find 10% of £240. This is easy as you just divide by 10. So £240 ÷ 10 = £24.

Then you simply halve £24 to find 5% since this is half of 10%. So £24 ÷ 2 = £12.

Now add £24 and £12 to make 15% which gives £36 and this is the answer you mark on the answer grid.

LESSON 15 PART 1

My Time My Score

Now look at the questions below. Work out your answers on some scrap paper and then mark them on the corresponding answer grids. Mark your time in the box provided when you've finished. Remember to get an adult to mark your answers. Then write your score in the box at the top of this page.

You have 10 minutes to complete these, so work quickly.

1. If a factory makes 1,220 cars and 10% are green. How many are green?

2. 50% of a restaurant's 64 tables have 4 seats. How many is this?

3. Of 860 passengers on a ferry, 20% travel alone. How many do not travel alone?

4. A savings account earns 2% on £450. How much money is this?

5. A new blouse costs £48 but is reduced by 10% in a sale. What is its new price?

6. Barak scored 75% on his maths test. If the test was out of 40, what was his actual score?

7. A golfer has 75 balls in his bag but loses 4% in the lake. How many does he lose?

8. A hospital has 240 beds. If 25% are empty, how many are being used?

9. If 20% of shoppers in a supermarket 1 day had a reward card, and this was 89 shoppers, how many shoppers were there in the store that day?

10. Carl is 5% of the way through his book. If the book has 320 pages, how many has he read so far?

LESSON 15 PART 1: ANSWER SHEET

Mark your answer by putting a horizontal line in 1 of the boxes, as in the examples below.

Example 1:

230 ☐
25 ☐
225 ☐
50 ▬
200 ☐

Example 2:

£12 ☐
£24 ☐
£36 ▬
£48 ☐
£60 ☐

1
12.2 ☐
1.22 ☐
122 ☐
102 ☐
202 ☐

2
46 ☐
32 ☐
21 ☐
34 ☐
36 ☐

3
86 ☐
172 ☐
688 ☐
774 ☐
430 ☐

4
£5 ☐
£6 ☐
£7 ☐
£8 ☐
£9 ☐

5
£4.80 ☐
£44.40 ☐
£44.80 ☐
£43.40 ☐
£43.20 ☐

6
10 ☐
15 ☐
20 ☐
25 ☐
30 ☐

7
3 ☐
4 ☐
5 ☐
6 ☐
7 ☐

8
150 ☐
160 ☐
170 ☐
180 ☐
190 ☐

9
440 ☐
445 ☐
450 ☐
455 ☐
460 ☐

10
16 ☐
20 ☐
24 ☐
28 ☐
32 ☐

How Did You Do? Let's Find Out!

Remember, there is no self-marking in this book. Please get an adult to mark your answers.

If you scored 8 or more out of 10

This type of question should be one you score well on so if you got 8 or 9 you should try to improve on the next set of questions.

If you scored fewer than 8 out of 10

Check the questions you got wrong and then read the tips for speeding up before you move on to the next set of questions.

TIPS FOR SPEEDING UP

- Make sure you know all the factors of 100 thoroughly – this will save you valuable time with these questions and help you spot those you can use short cuts on.

- If you need to find out percentages which are multiples of 10 then find 10% first and simply multiply your answer up.

VOCABULARY BUILDER

Use this page to write down any new words you've learnt from this book. Look up the meaning of each in a dictionary so that you'll know what they mean in future.

New word	Meaning

LESSON 15 PART 2

My Time

My Score

Now let's try some more. Work out the questions on some scrap paper and then mark your answers on the corresponding grids. Write the time you took and your score in the boxes above once you've finished. Remember that an adult needs to mark these for you.

You have 10 minutes to complete these, so work quickly.

1. A coach trip lasted 2 hours and 20% of this time was spent having lunch. How much time was spent on lunch?

2. A printer prints 750 sheets of paper. If 4% are colour, how many are not printed in colour?

3. Olivia's internet bill is £28.40 but she is given a 5% discount for paying on time; how much is her new bill?

4. A train can carry 460 passengers. If 20% of the seats are empty for 1 journey, how many passengers are on board?

5. A farmer produces 620 boxes of fruit. Of these 25% are boxes of pears. How many boxes of pears are there?

6. A teacher calculates that 15% of her 40 pupils handed their homework in early. How many is this?

7. Remy has painted 40% of a 160m fence. How much is there left for him to paint?

8. A mobile phone shop offers a 22% discount on phones which cost £80. How much money does this save customers?

9. If a car fuel gauge shows that it is 25% full when it has 9 litres of petrol in its tank, how many litres can the car hold when its tank is completely full?

10. Of 150 passengers on a ferry, 8% do not have a car. How many is this?

LESSON 15 PART 2: ANSWER SHEET

Mark your answer by putting a horizontal line in 1 of the boxes, as in the examples below.

Example 1:

230 ☐
25 ☐
225 ☐
50 ▬
200 ☐

Example 2:

£12 ☐
£24 ☐
£36 ▬
£48 ☐
£60 ☐

1
20 minutes ☐
24 minutes ☐
28 minutes ☐
32 minutes ☐
36 minutes ☐

2
150 ☐
300 ☐
450 ☐
600 ☐
720 ☐

3
£1.42 ☐
£2.84 ☐
£4.26 ☐
£13.49 ☐
£26.98 ☐

4
46 ☐
92 ☐
368 ☐
184 ☐
226 ☐

5
135 ☐
140 ☐
145 ☐
150 ☐
155 ☐

6
5 ☐
6 ☐
7 ☐
8 ☐
9 ☐

7
4m ☐
10m ☐
96m ☐
30m ☐
64m ☐

8
£2.20 ☐
£4.40 ☐
£17.60 ☐
£19.80 ☐
£15.40 ☐

9
16 litres ☐
32 litres ☐
34 litres ☐
36 litres ☐
40 litres ☐

10
12 ☐
16 ☐
20 ☐
24 ☐
28 ☐

SCORE SHEET

To find a percentage of a mark out of 10, simply multiply your score by 10 – but you should know this already!

Lesson	part 1 score	part 1 percent	part 2 score	part 2 percent
1				
2				
3				
4				
5				
6				
7				
8				
9				
10				
11				
12				
13				
14				
15				
Average				

AND FINALLY...

Firstly, let me begin by saying 'well done'. You must have worked hard to complete this book, especially on top of your other homework from school!

Now that you've completed the second maths book in the Practise & Pass 11+ series, it's time to take stock. Take a look at your scores above and make a note of the types of question you found quite straightforward and scored well on and those that you found more difficult and didn't score so well on. For those you found tougher, practise again.

Make sure you read back over the methods for each question – these will serve you well during your examination and when you're ready move on to level three of the series to try some full-length tests. Don't forget, if you need help with non-verbal reasoning, verbal reasoning or English, there are books for each of those to help you prepare for your exams.

⇨ *Practise & Pass 11+ Level One: Discover English*
⇨ *Practise & Pass 11+ Level One: Discover Verbal Reasoning*
⇨ *Practise & Pass 11+ Level One: Discover Non-Verbal Reasoning*
⇨ *Practise & Pass 11+ Level Two: Develop English*
⇨ *Practise & Pass 11+ Level Two: Develop Verbal Reasoning*
⇨ *Practise & Pass 11+ Level Two: Develop Non-Verbal Reasoning*
⇨ *Practise & Pass 11+ Level Three: Practice Test Papers*

Keep working and good luck!

ANSWERS

LESSON 1: part 1
1. 1,240
2. 80
3. £438
4. 1,135ft
5. 767ml
6. 4,195 miles
7. 23cm
8. 69
9. 161
10. 11,055 miles

LESSON 1: part 2
1. 33
2. −10°C
3. £283
4. 1,894
5. 314
6. 1,060
7. 379,401
8. 88 miles
9. 660ml
10. 46ft

LESSON 2: part 1
1. 24
2. 10
3. 140
4. 8
5. 24
6. 210
7. 84
8. 48
9. 80
10. 20

LESSON 2: part 2
1. 14
2. ¼
3. 540
4. 21
5. 522
6. 16
7. 14
8. 4
9. 20
10. 30 minutes

LESSON 3: part 1
1. 60
2. 21cm
3. 72
4. 219
5. 12 litres
6. 32,000ft
7. 33 miles
8. £729
9. 24
10. 1.2 litres

LESSON 3: part 2
1. 77
2. 24
3. 1,352
4. 15
5. 49
6. 14
7. 48
8. 56
9. 12
10. 30 minutes

LESSON 4: part 1
1. $\frac{1}{3}$
2. $\frac{1}{5}$
3. $\frac{1}{4}$
4. $\frac{7}{13}$
5. $\frac{2}{5}$
6. $\frac{1}{4}$
7. $\frac{3}{7}$
8. $\frac{27}{28}$
9. $\frac{1}{4}$
10. $\frac{16}{25}$

LESSON 4: part 2
1. $\frac{4}{5}$
2. $\frac{1}{2}$
3. $\frac{2}{3}$
4. $\frac{2}{3}$
5. $\frac{7}{13}$
6. $\frac{1}{7}$
7. $\frac{1}{4}$
8. $\frac{1}{35}$
9. $\frac{4}{5}$
10. $\frac{7}{15}$

LESSON 5: part 1
1. 2,200,000
2. £4.00
3. 900
4. 1m 23.7s
5. 5.30m
6. 600ml
7. 25,000
8. 234.76mm
9. 1,200
10. 10,000

LESSON 5: part 2
1. £2,000
2. 24,000
3. 34,000
4. 9.0s
5. 37 miles
6. 8,400
7. 20,000
8. 31 million
9. 50,000
10. 27.84mm

LESSON 6: part 1
1. £0.31
2. 80%
3. 20%
4. 75%
5. 20%
6. 40%
7. 58%
8. 65 litres
9. 8%
10. 80

LESSON 6: part 2
1. 19
2. 14%
3. 0.25km
4. 200
5. 70%
6. 73%
7. 2,300
8. 65%
9. 25%
10. 75%

LESSON 7: part 1
1. $\frac{1}{5}$
2. $\frac{2}{25}$
3. $\frac{4}{25}$
4. $\frac{6}{25}$
5. $\frac{8}{25}$
6. $\frac{1}{5}$
7. $\frac{4}{15}$
8. $\frac{2}{15}$
9. $\frac{1}{10}$
10. 30%

LESSON 7: part 2
1. $\frac{9}{50}$
2. $\frac{6}{25}$
3. 14%
4. $\frac{4}{25}$

5. 7/25
6. 100%
7. ¼
8. ¼
9. 87.5%
10. impossible

LESSON 8: part 1
1. 6
2. 49
3. 21
4. 60
5. 3:4
6. 2:1
7. 189
8. 150
9. 24
10. 77

LESSON 8: part 2
1. 50
2. 21
3. 41
4. £36
5. 8 litres
6. 2:1
7. 12
8. 24
9. 4:3
10. 30

LESSON 9: part 1
1. 84p
2. £2.90
3. £117
4. 94
5. 60p
6. £5.85
7. 45km
8. 64kg
9. 1 hour
10. £2,100

LESSON 9: part 2
1. 320
2. £2.10
3. 36 minutes
4. 3kg
5. 16
6. £1.30
7. 21 miles
8. 77
9. 7
10. £1.68

LESSON 10: part 1
1. 105cm³
2. 216ft³
3. 2m
4. 96cm³
5. 6
6. 378m³
7. 6 litres
8. 5m
9. 8cm
10. 6

LESSON 10: part 2
1. 1,350cm³
2. 1,728ft³
3. 7m
4. 240cm³
5. 24
6. 2m³
7. 24cm³
8. 9m
9. 6cm
10. 70

LESSON 11: part 1
1. 221m²
2. 64km²
3. 27ft²
4. 68m²
5. 66m²
6. 70ft²
7. 105cm²
8. pq÷2
9. 65ft²
10. g+f+h+h+j+k

LESSON 11: part 2
1. 62m
2. 72cm²
3. 72ft
4. 128m²
5. 74cm
6. 42.5m²
7. 30ft²
8. 87.5cm²
9. 130m²
10. 66.5ft²

LESSON 12: part 1
1. 3
2. 19
3. 13
4. 8 and 11 years
5. 9 years
6. 123
7. 6
8. 8
9. panda
10. 8

LESSON 12: part 2
1. 15
2. yellow
3. 40
4. 40%
5. 4
6. 100
7. 180
8. piano, drum
9. 5
10. 62

LESSON 13: part 1
1. 2,613
2. 4,104
3. 2,047
4. 3,465
5. 9,072
6. 15,168
7. 35 litres
8. 60
9. £12,831
10. 234 miles

LESSON 13: part 2
1. 4,368
2. 457
3. 512
4. 42,066
5. 33kg
6. 462 litres
7. 2,338
8. 1,665
9. 64
10. 13,100

LESSON 14: part 1
1. 17km
2. 320ml
3. 7
4. 13
5. 34
6. 18
7. 283
8. £4.77
9. 38
10. blue

LESSON 14: part 2
1. 44km
2. £3.00
3. 86mph
4. 47 minutes
5. 865ft
6. 80kg
7. 245
8. £3.55
9. 13°C
10. 5.31

LESSON 15: part 1
1. 122
2. 32
3. 688
4. £9
5. £43.20
6. 30
7. 3
8. 180
9. 445
10. 16

LESSON 15: part 2
1. 24 minutes
2. 720
3. £26.98
4. 368
5. 155
6. 6
7. 96m
8. £17.60
9. 36 litres
10. 12